A TEXT BOOK OF
PHARMACEUTICAL ANALYSIS

1st B.Pharm. 1st semester
(As Per PCI New Delhi Regulation)

DR MP BHAGAT

BLUEROSE PUBLISHERS
India | U.K.

Copyright © Dr. M.P. Bhagat 2024

All rights reserved by author. No part of this publication may be reproduced, stored in a retrieval system or transmitted in any form or by any means, electronic, mechanical, photocopying, recording or otherwise, without the prior permission of the author. Although every precaution has been taken to verify the accuracy of the information contained herein, the publisher assumes no responsibility for any errors or omissions. No liability is assumed for damages that may result from the use of information contained within.

BlueRose Publishers takes no responsibility for any damages, losses, or liabilities that may arise from the use or misuse of the information, products, or services provided in this publication.

For permissions requests or inquiries regarding this publication,
please contact:

BLUEROSE PUBLISHERS
www.BlueRoseONE.com
info@bluerosepublishers.com
+91 8882 898 898
+4407342408967

ISBN: 978-93-5989-889-6

Cover design: Muskan Sachdeva
Typesetting: Pooja Sharma

First Edition: February 2024

PREFACE

A text book of Pharmaceutical Analysis deals with the fundamentals of analytical chemistry and principles of electrochemical analysis of drugs.

It also describes principles and methods of determination of different compounds under acid base, precipitation, non-aqueous, complexometric, gravimetric and redox titrations as per syllabus framed by Pharmacy Council of India, New Delhi.

This text book isalso useful to the students and teachers of Diploma in Pharmacy, Pharm.D courses.

I will be glad to receive comments and suggestions from readers so that book can be made more useful and meaningful in future.

I express my special thanks to Prof.(Dr.) M.D.karvekar, Pharmaceutical chemistry, for his sincere guidance.

I am very much thankful to our Honorable Secretary, Janab Taj Mohammed Khan, RMET, Mysore, for his suggestion.

I am most grateful to my wife, Mrs. Veena Bhagat, sons, Rakesh & Raveesh, daughter-in-laws, Pallavi &Neha and my lovable grand-sons, Rihaan and Ityam and grand-daughter Rhea for their sincere support.

I would like thank CIIT computers, Mysore, Mr. Tasdeeq Nizam, for helping in getting the book compiled and bring this in printing format.

I express my sincere thanks to Blue Rose Publishers for publishing this book promptly.

Dr. M.P Bhagat

PHARMACEUTICAL ANALYSIS (Theory)

45 Hours

COURSE CONTENT

Unit – I **10 Hours**

(a) Pharmaceutical analysis: --Definition and scope

(i) Different techniques of analysis

(ii) Methods of expressing concentration

(iii) Primary and Secondary standards.

(iv) Preparation and standardization of various molar and normal solution:--

Oxalic acid , sodium hydroxide , hydrochloric acid , sodium thiosulphate, sulphuric acid, potassium permanganate and ceric ammonium sulphate

(b) Errors:-- Source of errors , types of errors , methods of minimizing errors, accuracy , precision and significant figures

UNIT – II **10 Hours**

Acid base titration:-- Theories of acid base indicators , classification of acid base titration and theory involved in titration of strong , weak ,and very weak acids and bases , neutralization curves

Non aqueous titration:-- Solvents , acidimetry and alkalimetry titration and estimation of sodium benzoate and Ephedrine HCL

UNIT – III **10 Hours**

Precipitation titrations:-- Mohr's method , Volhard 's , modified Volhard's , Fajans method , estimation of sodium chloride.

Complexometric titration:-- Classification , metal ion indicators , masking and demasking reagents , estimation of sodium chloride .

Gravimetry:-- Principle and steps involved in gravimetric analysis . Purity of the precipitate : co-precipitation and post precipitation , Estimation of barium Sulphate.

UNIT –IV **08 Hours**

Redox titrations

(a) Concepts of oxidation and reduction

(b) Types of redox titrations (principles and applications)

Cerimetry , Iodimetry , Iodometry ,Bromatometry, Dichrometry , Titration with Potassium iodate

UNIT – V **07 Hours**

Electrochemical methods of analysis

Conductometry:-- Introduction , conductivity cell , conductometric titrations , applications .

Potentiometry:-- Electrochemical cell , construction and working of reference (Standard hydrogen , silver chloride electrode and calomel electrode) and indicator electrodes (metal electrodes and glass electrode), methods to determine and point of potentiometric titration and applications .

Polarography:--Principle , Ilkovic equation , construction and working of dropping mercury electrode and rotating platinum electrode , applications

Contents

UNIT-I 10 Hours

(a) PHARMACEUTICAL ANALYSIS:-- 2
(i) DIFFERENT TECHNIQUES OF ANALYSIS:-- 2
(ii) METHODS OF EXPRESSING CONCENTRATION:-- 4
(iii) PRIMARY AND SECONDARY STANDARDS:-- 7
(iv) PREPARATION AND STANDARDISATION OF VARIOUS MOLAR AND NORMAL SOLUTIONS:-- 9
(b) ERRORS 15

UNIT-II 10 Hours

(a) ACID BASE TITRATION 22
(b) NON AQUEOUS TITRATION:- 35

UNIT-III 10 Hours

(a) PRECIPITATION TITRATIONS:-- 44
(b) COMPLEXOMETRIC TITRATION:-- 57
GRAVIMETRY:- 69

UNIT-IV 8 Hours

REDOX TITRATIONS:-- 78
(a) CONCEPTS OF OXIDATION AND REDUCTION OR REDOX REACTION:-- ... 78
(b) TYPES OF REDOX REACTION:-- 82

UNIT-V 7 Hours

ELECTROCHEMICAL METHODS OF ANALYSIS:-- 104
(a) CONDUCTOMETRY:-- 104
(b) POTENTIOMETRY 123
(c) POLAROGRAPHY:-- 142

UNIT-I

(a) PHARMACEUTICAL ANALYSIS:--

DEFINITION:--

Pharmaceutical analysis isbranch of chemistry which is used to identify,separate and purify the substances.It is used to determine ingredients, presence of impurities and excipients in pharmaceutical products and also used to determine uniformity, solubility and dissolution rate for such substances which are generally obtained from animals, plants, microbes, minerals **and**synthetic chemicals.

Pharmaceutical analysis focuses on accessing the quantities and qualities of drugs and their impurities in development processes.

It is also used for the separation of components from the mixture and for the determination of the structure of the compounds.

SCOPE OR APPLICATIONOF PHARMACEUTICAL ANALYSIS:--

(1) Pharmaceutical analysis is basically used for the purpose of classification of compound according to its chemical properties.

(2) It is used for analysis of mixtures of compounds.

(3) It is used for the purpose of separation of components from mixture.

(4) It is used for purpose of purification, identification and characterization of compounds.

(5) It is also used to determine the quality and quantity of raw materials and finished products or formulations by using different methods of analysis.

(i) DIFFERENT TECHNIQUES OF ANALYSIS:--

It can be divided into two major categories:--

(1) QUALITATIVE ANALYSIS:--

(2) QUANTITATIVE ANALYSIS:--

(1) QUALITATIVE ANALYSIS:--

It is such type of analysis which is used to analyze the presence or absence of certain substances in unknown sample.

For example,Colour reaction test, test for purity, limit test, melting point and boiling point.

(2) QUANTITATIVE ANALYSIS:--

It is such type of analysis which is used to determine the quantity of any compound or substance present in the sample.

Quantitative analysis is based upon quantitative performance of suitable chemical reactions. It either measures the amount of reagent needed to complete the reaction or ascertains the amount of reaction product obtained.

TYPES OF PHARMACEUTICAL ANALYSIS:--

(1) QUALITATIVE ANALYSIS:--

It is such type of analysis which is used to determine the composition of natural and synthetic products. It is used to indicate whether the substance or compound is present in the sample or not. It is also used for detection of evolved gas, for formation of precipitate, limit tests, colour change reactions, melting point and boiling point.

(2) QUANTITATIVE ANALYSIS:--

It is used to quantify any compound or substance in the sample by the use of different methods like

(a) gravimetric analysis.

(b) appropriate electrical measurements, for example, Potentiometry.

(c) the measurement of certain optical properties, for example; absorption spectra.

(d) in some cases like a combination of optical or electrical measurement and quantitative chemical reaction, for example, amperometric titration.

VARIOUS TYPES OF QUALITATIVE ANALYSIS:--

(1) Chemical method

(a) Volumetric or titrimetric method

(b) Gravimetric method

(2) Instrumental method

(3) Microbiological method

(4) Biological method

(1) CHEMICAL METHOD:--

(a) VOLUMETRIC METHOD:--

It is such type of method which is used to find out the volume or strength or normality or weight of unknown substance or solution by the help of strength of known substance or solution by finding out the volume of consumed solution by means of titration in the presence of suitable medium and indicator.

Further by applying certain $N_1V_1 = N_2V_2$ formula,

the normality or strength can be determined,

where N_1, N_2 are normality of unknown and known solution and

V_1, V_2 are taken volume and consumed volume of the solution.

Volumetric analysis can be subdivided into following methods or titrations:--

(1) Neutralization titration

(2) Non aqueous titration

(3) Redox titration

(4) Precipitation titration

(5) Complexometric titration

(b) GRAVIMETRIC METHOD:--

It is such type of method which is used to find out the weight of compounds by isolating and weighing of compounds by means of precipitation or volatilization method of analysis and converting them into pure form of compound.

Further with the help of known weights of constituents, presence of unknown substance can be calculated.

(2) INSTRUMENTAL METHOD:--

It is such type of method which is used to analyze the physical or chemical property of compound by the use of known strength of compound.

(3) MICROBIOLOGICAL METHOD:--

It is used for such type of compounds which are used for determination of inhibition of growth of bacteria by the substance to be analyzed in comparison with the standard compounds on the basis of result in respect of therapeutic efficacy of antibiotics.

(4) BIOLOGICAL METHOD:--

It is such type of method which is used to observe the biological effect of drug on some type of living matter. It is used to estimate the potency of drug.

It is also used to measure various parameters including weight of tissue of organ, weight of organs of blood, parameters such as blood, glucose, cholesterol, urea, enzyme etc.,

(ii) METHODS OF EXPRESSING CONCENTRATION:--

The concentration of solutions can be expressed quantitatively by different methods:--

(I) MASS PERCENTAGE (w/w):--

The mass percentage of a component can be defined as

Mass% of a component = $\dfrac{\text{Mass of the component in the solution}}{\text{Total mass of the solution}} \times 100$

For example,

If a solution is described by 10% glucose in water by mass, it means that 10g of glucose is dissolved in 90g of water resulting in a 100g solution.

Concentration described by mass percentage is commonly used in industrial chemical applications.

For example, commercial bleaching solution contains 3.62 mass percentage of sodium hypochlorite in water.

(II) VOLUME PERCENTAGE:--

The volume percentage can be defined as

Volume % of a component = $\dfrac{\text{Volume of the component}}{\text{Total volume of solution}} \times 100$

For example,

10% ethanol solution in water means that 10ml. of ethanol is diluted to total volume of 100 ml by using 90 ml of water.

Solutions containing liquids are commonly expressed in this unit.

For example, a 35%(v/v) solution of ethylene glycol is used in cars for cooling the engine.

At this concentration the antifereeze lowers the freezing pont of water to 255.4K (-17.6°C).

(III) MASS BY VOLUME PERCENTAGE(w/v):--

Mass by valume percentage is commonly used in medicine and pharmacy.

It is the mass of the solute dissolved in 100 ml. of the solution.

(IV) PARTS PER MILLION:--

When a solute is present in trace quantities then it is convenient to express concentration in parts per million (ppm).

Parts per million can be defined as

Parts per million = $\dfrac{\text{Number of parts of the component}}{\text{Total number of parts of all components of the solution}} \times 10^6$

Note:--

As in the case of percentage, concentration in parts per million can also be expressed as mass to mass, volume to volume and mass to volume.

A litre of sea water (which weighs 1030g) contains about 6×10^{-3} g of dissolved oxygen.

Such a small concentration is also expressed as 5.8g per 10^6g (5.8ppm) of sea water.

The concentration of pollutants in water or atmosphere is often expressed in terms of µg mL^{-1} or ppm.

(V) MOLE FRACTION:--

Mole fraction of a component can be defined as

$$\text{Mole fraction of a component} = \frac{Number\ of\ moles\ of\ the\ component}{Total\ number\ of\ moles\ of\ all\ the\ components}$$

Mole fraction is commonly used by the use of symbol x and subscript used on the right hand side of x denotes the component.

For example,

In a binary mixture, if the number of moles of A and B are nA and nB respectively, the mole fraction of A will be

$$xA = \frac{nA}{nA + nB}$$

For a solution containing i number of components,

we have

$$x_i = \frac{n_1}{n_1 + n_2 + n_3 - - - - - + n_i} = \frac{n_1}{\sum n_i}$$

It can be shown that in a given solution sum of all the mole fractions is unity i.e.,

$$x_1 + x_2 + - - - - - - - - - + x_i = 1$$

Mole fraction unit is very useful in relating some physical properties of solution, say vapour pressure with the concentration of the solution and quite useful in describing the calculations involving gas mixtures.

(VI) MOLARITY:--

Molarity(M) is defined as number of moles of solute dissolved in one litre (or one cubic decimeter) of solution.

$$Molarity = \frac{Moles\ of\ solute}{Volume\ of\ solution\ in\ litre}$$

For example,

0.25MolL^{-1} (or 0.25M) solution of NaOH means that 0.25mol of NaOH has been dissolved in one litre (or one cubic decimeter) water.

(VII) MOLALITY:--

Molality (m) is defined as the number of moles of the solute per kilogram (Kg) of the solvent.

It can be expressed as

$$Molality\ (m) = \frac{Moles\ of\ solute}{Mass\ of\ solvent\ in\ Kg}$$

For example, 1.00 mol Kg^{-1} (or 1.00m) solution of KCl means that 1 mol (74.5g) of KCl is dissolved in Kg of water.

Each method of expressing concentration of the solutions has its own merits and demerits. Mass percentage, mole fraction and molality are independent of temperature whereas molarity is a function of temperature. This is because volume depends on temperature and the mass does not.

(iii) PRIMARY AND SECONDARY STANDARDS:--

PRIMARY STANDARDS:--

Primary standards are such type of substances which are available in a pure state and their solution of definite normality can be prepared by weighing out an equivalent or a definite fraction by dissolving it in the solvent usually water and making up the solution to a known volume.

In practice a little more concentrated solution is prepared and then it is diluted with distilled water until the desired normality is obtained.

For example,

If N_1 = required normality,

V_1 = volume after dilution,

N_2 = the normality originally obtained,

and V_2 = the original volume taken.

then by applying following formula,

V_1 or volume after dilution can be calculated.

$N_1V_1 = N_2V_2$

Or,

$$V_1 = \frac{N_2 V_2}{N_1}$$

Examples of primary standards in different reactions can be listed as such:--

(i) ACID BASE REACTIONS:--

Sodium carbonate, sodium tetraborate, potassium hydrogen phthalate, constant-boiling point hydrochloric acid, potassium hydrogen iodate, benzoic acid.

(ii) COMPLEX FORMATION REACTIONS:--

Silver, silver nitrate, sodium chloride, various metals like zinc, magnesium, copper and spectrocopically pure manganese and salts depending upon the reaction used.

(iii) PRECIPITATION REACTIONS:--

Silver, silver nitrate, sodium chloride, potassium chloride and potassium bromide.

(iv) REDOX REACTIONS:--

Potassium dichromate, potassium bromate, potassium iodate, potassium hydrogen iodate, iodine, sodium oxalate, arsenic (III) oxide and pure iron.

SECONDARY STANDARDS:--

Seconday standards are such type of substances which are not available in pure state and their normality can be obtained approximately and definite normality can be calculated by means of standardization with primary standard substances.

Examples:--

(1) ACID BASE REACTIONS:--

Sodium hydroxide, potassium hydroxide, hydrochloric acid.

(ii) REDOX REACTIONS:--

Potassium permanganate, sodium thiosulphate, hydrogen peroxide.

(iii) COMPLEX FORMATION REACTION:--

Disodium EDTA

(iv) PRECIPITATION REACTIONS:--

Ammonium thiocyanate.

REUIREMENTS FOR IDEAL PRIMARY STANDARD

Or,

REUISITIES OF PRIMARY STANDARD:--

(1) Primary standard must be easy to obtain, to purify, to dry (preferably at 110 - 120°C) and to preserve in a pure state.

(2) The substance should be unaltered in air during weighing. Hence, it should not be hygroscopic nor oxidized by air nor affected by carbon dioxide. It should maintain its composition and should be unchanged during storage.

(3) The substance should be capable of being tested for impurities by qualitative and other tests of known sensitivity. The total amount of impurities should not exceed 0.01-0.02 percent.

(4) It should have a high equivalent so that the weighing errors may be negligible.

(5) The substance should be readily soluble under the conditions in which it is employed.

(6) The reaction with the standard solution should be stoichiometric and practically instantancous. The titration error should be negligible or easy to determine accurately by experiment.

(iv) PREPARATION AND STANDARDISATION OF VARIOUS MOLAR AND NORMAL SOLUTIONS:--

(1) OXALIC ACID:--

Oxalic acid, 0.1N:--6.3g of oxalic acid is dissolved in 1.0 liter of water.

ASSAY:--

Oxalic acid is used as primary standard substance. It is available in pure form. So, it is used for standardization of other secondary standard solution like 0.1N NaOH or 0.1 N KMnO4 solution.

So, oxalic acid can be assayed with the help of following two methods:--

(1) ACID BASE TITRATION METHOD:--

Oxalic acid can be assayed with the help of acid-base titration method by using 0.1N NaOH solution.

During the process of the assay, oxalic acid reacts with sodium hydroxide solution in the presence of phenolphthalein as indicator and sodium oxalate is produced at the end of the reaction. At the end point, a pink color is obtained.

By the use of following formula and consumed volume of 0.1N NaOH solution, percentage purity of oxalic acid can be determined.

% Purity of oxalic acid

$$= \frac{Consumed\ volume\ of\ 0.1NaOH\ \times Normality\ of\ NaOH\ \times 0.063}{0.1\ \times Weight\ of\ oxalic\ acid} \times 100$$

REACTION:-- $H_2C_2O_4 + 2NaOH = Na_2C_2O_4 + 2H_2O$

PROCESS:--

0.1g of oxalic acid is taken in a conical flask and dissolved in 10ml. of water. Further 1 or 2 drops of phenolphthalein indicator is added and titrated with 0.1N NaOH solution. At the end point a pink colour is obtained.

Each ml. of 0.1N NaOH is equivalent to 0.063 g of oxalic acid

(2) REDOX TITRATION METHOD:--

Oxalic acid also can be assayed by the help of redox titration method by the use of 0.1 N $KMnO_4$ solution.

During the process of the assay, oxalic acid solution is heated at temperature of 60-70°C to get complete oxidation of oxalic acid into carbondioxide. Further in hot condition only it is titrated with 0.1N $KMnO_4$ solution in the presence of dilute H_2SO_4 acid solution. Here $KMnO_4$ acts as self redox indicator. At end point a pink colour is obtained.

During the process of assay, oxalic acid acts as reducing agent which oxidizes into carbon dioxide with the loss of two number of electrons where as $KMnO_4$ acts as oxidizing agent and reduces into manganese sulphate with the gain of two number of electrons.

With the help of consumed volume of 0.1N $KMnO_4$ solution and IP factor, Percentage purity of oxalic acid can be determined.

$$\% \; Purity \; of \; oxalic \; acid = \frac{Volume \; of \; 0.1N \; KMnO_4 \times Normality \; of \; 0.1N \; KMnO_4 \times 0.063}{0.1 \times Wt \; of \; Oxalic \; acid} \times 100$$

REACTION:--

$2KMnO_4 + 5H_2C_2O_4, 2H_2O + 3H_2SO_4 = K_2SO_4 + 2MnSO_4 + 10CO_2 + 18H_2O$

PROCESS:--

0.1g of oxalic acid is taken in a conical flask and dissolved in 10ml. of water. Then 10ml. of dilute sulphuric acid is added. Further it is heated at temperature of 60-70°C. In hot condition only it is titrated with 0.1N $KMnO_4$. At end point a pink colour is obtained. Finally consumed volume of 0.1N $KMnO_4$ is noted.

Each ml. of 0.1N $KMnO_4$ is equivalent to 0.063g of oxalic acid.

(2) SODIUM HYDROXIDE:--

Sodium hydroxide, 1M:--

42g of sodium hydroxide is dissolved in sufficient carbon dioxide-free water to produce 1000 ml.

STANDARDISATION:--

Sodium hydroxide 1M solution can be standardized by the use of acid base titration method by using Potassium hydrogen phthalate in the presence of phenolphthalein indicator.

During the process of standardization sodium hydroxide reacts with potassium hydrogen phthalate and forms sodium potassium phthalate by producing a pink colour atthe end of the reaction.

By the use of consumed volume of 1M NaOH solution and IP factor, exact molarity of sodium hydroxide can be calculated.

$$\text{Molarity of NaOH} = \frac{\text{Weight of potassium hydrogen phthalate}}{\text{Volume of 1M NaOH} \times 0.2042}$$

REACTION:--

$KHC_8H_4O_4 + NaOH = KNaC_8H_4O_4 + H_2O$

PROCESS:--

About 5.0g of potassium hydrogen phthate is powdered, dried at 120°C for 2 hours and dissolved in 75ml. of carbon dioxide-free water. Then 0.1ml. of phenolphthalein solution is added and titrated with sodium hydroxide 1M solution until a permanent pink colour is produced.

Each ml. of 1M sodium hydroxide is equivalent to 0.2042 g of $C_8H_5KO_4$.

(3) HYDROCHLORIC ACID:--

Hydrochloric acid, 1M:--

85ml. of HCl is diluted with water to produce 1000ml.

STANDARDISATION:--

Hydrochloric acid solution, 1M can be standardized by the help of acid-base titration method by using anhydrous sodium carbonate in the presence of methyl red as indicator.

During the process of standardization, hydrochloric acid reacts with anhydrous sodium carbonate in the presence of methylred as indicator and sodium chloride is produced at the end of the reaction.

By the use of following formula, consumed volume of titrant hydrochloric acid solution and I.P factor, exact molarity of HCl can be determined.

$$\text{Molarity of HCl} = \frac{\text{weight of anhdrous sodium carbonate}}{\text{Consumed volume of 1M HCl} \times 0.05299}$$

REACTION:--

$2HCl + Na_2CO_3 = 2NaCl + H_2O + CO_2$

PROCESS:--

1.5g of anhydrous sodium carbonate is heated at about 270°C for 1 hour. Then it is dissolved in 100ml. of water. Further 0.1ml. of methyl red solution is added.

After that it is titrated with 1M hydrochloric acid solution taken in a burette until the solution becomes faintly pink.

Solution is heated to boiling, cooled and titration is continued. It is again heated to boiling and titrated further as necessary until the faint pink colour is no longer affected by continued boiling.

Each ml. of 1M HCl is equivalent to 0.05299 g of $Na_2C_2O_3$.

(4) SODIUM THIOSULPHATE:--

Sodium thiosulphate, 0.1 M:--

25g of sodium thiosulphate and 0.2g of sodium carbonate are dissolved in carbon dioxide-free water and diluted to 1000ml. with the same solvent.

STANDARDISATION:--

Sodium thiosulphate can be standardized by the help of bromometry redox titration method by using potassium bromate in the presence of starch solution as indicator.

During the process of standardization, sodium thiosulphate reacts with potassium bromate in the presence of potassium iodide and hydrochloric acid and iodine gets liberated. The liberated iodine reacts with sodium thiosulphate solution and provides sodium tetrathionate and sodium iodide. At the end-point colour changes from blue to colourless.

With the help of consumed volume of sodium thiosulphate, 0.1M solution and I.P factor, exact molarity of sodium thiosulphate can be determined.

$$\text{Molarity of sodium thiosulphate} = \frac{\text{Weight of potassium bromate}}{\text{Consumed volume of 0.1M sodium thiosulphate}} \times 0.002784$$

REACTION:--

$BrO_3^- + 5I^- + 6H^+ = 3I_2 + 3H_2O$

$I_2 + 2Na_2S_2O_3 = 2NaI + Na_2S_4O_6$

PROCESS:--

0.2g of potassium bromate is dissolved in sufficient water to produce 250ml. 0.2 g of potassium iodide and 3ml. of 2M hydrochloric acid are added to 50ml. of this solution.

Further it is titrated with the sodium thiosulphate solution using starch solution as indicator till blue colour gets discharged.

Each ml. of 0.1M sodium thiosulphate is equivalent to 0.002784g of $KBrO_3$

(5) SULPHURIC ACID:--

Sulphuric acid, 0.5M:--

30ml. of sulphuric acid is added slowly with stirring to about 1000ml. of water. Then it is allowed to cool to 25°C.

STANDARDISATION:--

Sulphuric acid, 0.5M can be standardized with the help of anhydrous sodium carbonate as described under the standardization of 1M hydrochloric acid.

Each ml. of 0.5M sulphuric acid is equivalent to 0.05299g of Na_2CO_3.

REACTION:--

$H_2SO_4 + Na_2CO_3 = Na_2SO_4 + H_2O + CO_2$

(6) POTASSIUM PERMANGANATE:--

Potassium permanganate, 0.02M:--

3.2g of potassium permanganate is dissolved in 1000ml. of water and heated on a water-bath for 1 hour. Then it is allowed to stand for 2 days. Further it is filtered through glass wool.

STANDARDISATION:--

Potassium permanganate can be standardized by the use of iodometry redox titration method with the use of 0.1M sodium thiosulphate solution in the presence of potassium iodide, sulphuric acid and starch solution as indicator.

During the process of standardization potassium permanganate reacts with potassium iodide and sulphuric acid and iodine gets liberated. Then liberated iodine reacts with sodium thiosulphate solution and provides sodium iodide alongwith sodium tetrathionate. At the end point a blue colour is obtained.

By the use of consumed volume of 0.1M sodium thiosulphate and I.P factor, exact molarity of potassium permanganate can be determined.

$$Molarity\ of\ Potassium\ permanganate = \frac{Weight\ of\ KMnO_4}{Consumed\ volume\ of\ Na_2S_2O_3} \times .003161$$

REACTION:--

$2KMnO_4 + 10KI + 8H_2SO_4 \rightarrow 6K_2SO_4 + 2MnSO_4 + 5I_2 + 8H_2O$

$I_2 + 2Na_2S_2O_3 = 2NaI + Na_2S_4O_6$

PROCESS:--

2g of potassium iodide is added to 25ml. of 0.02M potassium permanganate solution in a glass-stoppered flask. Then 10ml. of 1M sulphuric acid is added. After that liberated iodine is titrated with 0.1M sodium thiosulphate by using 3ml. of starch solution as indicator. Further determination is performed and any necessary correction is made.

Each ml. of 0.1M sodium thiosulphate is equivalent to 0.003161g of $KMnO_4$.

(7) CERIC AMMONIUM SULPHATE:--

Ceric ammonium sulphate, 0.1M:--

65g of ceric ammonium sulphate is dissolved in a mixture of 30ml. of sulphuric acid and 500ml. of water with the aid of gentle heat. Then it is cooled and solution is filtered if it is turbid. After that it is diluted to 1000ml. with water.

STANDARDISATION:--

Ceric ammonium sulphate, 0.1M can be standardized by the use of redox titration method by using arsenic trioxide in the presence of sulphuric acid and ferroin sulphate solution as indicator.

During the process of standardization arsenic trioxide reacts with sodium hydroxide, sulphuric acid and osmic acid solution. Then it is titrated with ceric ammonium sulphate in the presence of ferroin sulphate indicator. At the end of titration ceric ammonium sulphate reduces into cerous ammonium sulphate whereas arsenic trioxide converts into arsenious acid and finally into arsenic acid.

With the help of consumed volume of ceric ammonium sulphate solution and I.P factor, exact molarity of ceric ammonium sulphate can be determined.

$$Molarity\ of\ Ceric\ ammonium\ sulphate = \frac{Weight\ of\ arsenic\ trioxide}{Consumed\ volume\ of\ ceric\ ammonium\ sulphate \times 0.004946}$$

REACTION:--

$As_2O_3 + 3H_2O = 2H_3AsO_3$

$2Ce^{4+} + H_3AsO_3 + H_2O = 2Ce^{3+} + H_3AsO_4 + 2H^+$

PROCESS:--

About 0.2g of arsenic trioxide is dried at 105°c for 1 hour and transferred to a 500ml. conical flask. Then inner wall of the flask is washed down with 25ml. of a 8.0% w/v solution of sodium hydroxide. It is stirred to dissolve.

After that 100ml. of water is added and mixed. Then 30ml. of dilute sulphuric acid, 0.15ml. of osmic acid solution and 0.1ml. of ferroin sulphate solution are added. Further it is slowly titrated with the ceric ammonium sulphate solution until the pink colour is changed to a very pale blue by adding the titrant slowly towards the end point.

Each ml. of 0.1M ceric ammonium sulphate is equivalent to 0.004946 g of AS_2O_3.

(b) ERRORS

Or,

ERROR OF QUANTITATIVE DETERMINATION

Or,

ANALYTICAL ERROR:--

Error is the result of quantitative determination or analysis which always differs to some extent from true value eventhough quantitative determination is carried out carefully or performed with the help of correct application of analytical process. Error affects an experimental result.

CLASSIFICATION OF ERRORS

Or,

SOURCES OF ERRORS

Or,

TYPES OF ERRORS

Error can be classified into three types:--

(1) DETERMINATE ERROR OR CONSTANT ERROR OR SYSTEMATIC ERROR

(2) INDETERMINATE ERROR OR ACCIDENTAL ERROR OR RANDOM ERROR

(3) MISTAKES

(1) DETERMINATE ERROR:--

Determinate error is such type of error which is constant in magnitude or vary in accordance with a definite law.

Determinate error can be avoided or whose magnitude can be determined.

Determinate error can be classified further into following types:--

(1) Operational and personal error

(2) Insturmental and reagent error

(3)Errors of method

(4) Additive and proportional error

(1) OPERATIONAL AND PERSONAL ERROR:--

OPERATIONAL ERROR:--

It is due to individual analyst irresponsibility.

Operational errors are mostly physical in nature and occur when sound analytical technique is not followed.

Examples:--

(a) Use of reagents containing harmful impurities

(b) Mechanical loss of materials in various steps of an analysis

(c) Underwashing or overwashing of precipitates

(d) Ignition of precipitate at incorrect temperature

(e) Insufficient cooling of crucibles before weighing

PERSONAL ERROR:--

It may arise from the constitutional inability of an individual to make certain observation accurately.

Example:--

Some persons are unable to judge colour changes sharply in visual titrations which may result in a slight overstepping of end-point.

(2) INSTRUMENTAL AND REAGENT ERROR:--

Instrumental error may arise from faulty construction of balances, use of uncalibrated weights and graduated glasswares.

Reagent error may arise from the attack of reagents on glassware, porcelain; volatilization of platinum at very high temperature and from the use of reagents containing impurities.

(3) ERRORS OF METHOD:--

They may arise from incorrect sampling.

Examples:--

(1) Errors may arise from co-precipitation, post-precipitation, decomposition of weighing forms on ingnition in gravimetric analtsis. They may arise from incompleteness of a reaction.

(ii) In titrimetric analysis errors may arise due to failure of reactions to proceed the completion of the reaction of substances other than the constituent being determined and a diference between the observed end point and the stoichiometric end point of a reaction.

(4) ADDITIVE AND PROPORTIONAL ERROR:--

Absolute value of an additive error is independent of the amount of the constituent present in the determination.

Example:--

Loss in weight of a crucible in which a precipitate is ignited and errors in weights.

Absolute value of a proportional error depends upon the amount of the constituent.

Proportional error may arise from an impurity in a standard substance which leads to an incorrect value for the normality of a standard solution.

(2) INDETERMINATE ERROR:--

It is such type of error which is not constant in magnitude or may not vary in accordance with a definite law.

Indeterminate error can not be avoided or prevented or eliminated by corrections.

Indeterminate error may produce by slight variations which may occur in successive measurements made by the same observer with the greatest care under as nearly identical conditions as possible.

Indeterminate error may arise due to such cause where analyst may not have control.

During the process of quantitative analysis when large number of observations is taken then small error may occur frequently than large ones and large errors occur relatively infrequently.

(3) MISTAKES:--

Misktake is a type of crude error which generally turns the analytical result. Mistake can be caused due to incorrect counting of weights or wrong readings on the scale in weighing, wrong burette reading in titration or by overflow of the solution or precipitate during the determination of the unknown substance.

Mistake can be minimized by taking average of a series of determination during the analysis.

MINIMIZATION OF ERRORS

Or,

REDUCTION OF ERRORS:--

Determinate errors can be minimized by the use of following methods:--

(1) Calibration of apparatus and application of corrections

(2) Running a blank determination

(3) Running a control determination

(4) Use of independent method of analysis

(5) Running of parallel determinations

(6) Standard addition

(7) Internal standards

(8) Amplification methods

(9) Isotopic dilution

(1) CALIBRATION OF APPARATUS AND APPLICATION OF CORRECTIONS:--

All instruments like weights, flasks, burettes, pipettes should be calibrated and appropriate corrections can be applied to the original instruments and likely error can be minimized.

(2) RUNNING A BLANK DETERMINATION:--

Blank determination is generally used to find out the effect of impurities introduced through the reagents and vessels or to determine the excess of standard solution necessary to establish the end point under the condition generally used in the titration of unknown sample.

During the process of blank determination, a separate determination is carried out by omitting the sample under the same experimental condition which is employed in actual analysis of the sample and like this amount of error can be minimised.

(3) RUNNING A CONTROL DETERMINATION:--

During the process of control determination certain standard substances or primary standard substances like sodium oxalate, benzoic acid, arsenic trioxide can be used.

Control determination is carried out under same identical experimental condition which is used for a quantity of standard substance and standard substance contains the same weight of the constituent as it is contained in unknown sample.

The weight of the constituent in unknown sample can be calculated with the help of following relation.

$$\frac{result\ found\ for\ standard}{result\ found\ for\ unknown} = \frac{weight\ of\ constituent\ in\ standard}{x}$$

where x = weight of constituent in unknown.

Thus by use of control determination error can be minimized.

(4) USE OF INDEPENDENT METHODS OF ANALYSIS:--

Error can be minimized by the use of independent methods of analysis.

For example, iron can be determined by means of gravimetric method or by use of titrimetric method.

During the process of gravimetric method, iron is converted into ferric hydroxide by the use of precipitation method of analysis. After that it is converted into ferric oxide by means of ignition.

During the process of titrimetric analysis iron is reduced into ferric state in the presence of dilute sulphuric acid medium and further titrated with standard solution of ceric ammonium sulphate by the use of ferroin solution as indicator.

If result obtained by the above two methods are concordant, then values are found correct within small limits of error.

(5) RUNNING OF PARALLEL DETERMINATIONS:--

A parallel determination is used to make a check on the result of a single determination.

If values of parallel determination is too small or vary by more than three parts per thousand then determination is repeated until satisfactory concordance is obtained by getting duplicate or triplicate determination.

Like this error can be minimized by the use of parallel determination.

(6) STANDARD ADDITION:--

Standard addition is used in case of polarography and spectrophotometry.

During the process of standard addition, a known amount of the constituent (being determined) is added to the sample which is analysed for total amount of constituent present.

The difference between the analytical result for samples with and without the added constituent gives the recovery of the amount of added constituent.

If the recovery is satisfactory then accuracy of the method gets enhanced.

(7) INTERNAL STANDARDS:--

Internal standards method is used in case of spectroscopic and chromatographic determinations.

Internal standards method involves the addition of a fixed amount of internal standard (reference material) to a series of known concentrations of the material (to be measured).

The ratios of physical value (absorption or peak size) of internal standard and series of known concentrations is plotted against the concentration values. This should give a straight line.

Any unknown concentration can be determined by adding same quantity of internal standard and finding whether the ratio obtained falls on the concentration scale.

(8) AMPLIFICATION METHOD:--

Amplification method can be used for the determination of very small amount of the material and during the determination small amount of material can be reacted in such a way that every molecule produces two or more molecules of some other measurable material i.e., amplification of quantity gets completed. Like this error can be minimized.

(9) ISOTOPIC DILUTION:--

During the process of isotopic dilution, known amount of the element (being determined) containing a radioactive isotope, is mixed with the sample and the element is isolated in a pure from which is weighed.

The radioactivity of the isolated element is measured and compared with that of the added element; the weight of the element in the sample can then be calculated. Like this error can be minimized.

ACCURACY AND PRECISION:--

ACCURACY:--

Accuracy of a determination can be defined as the concordance between it and the true or most probable value.

Accuracy is the agreement of a particular value to the true value of the result.

Accuracy expresses the correctness of a measurement.

PRECISION:--

Precision can be defined as the concordance of a series of measurements of the same quantity.

Precision can be measured by the use of mean deviation or relative mean deviation.

Precision rarely exceeds 1 to 2 parts per thousand in quantitative analysis.

Precision expresses the reproducibility of a measurement.

Precision always accompanies accuracy but high degree of precision does not imply accuracy.

Precision refers to the closeness of various measurement for the same quantity.

Accuracy and precision can be explained by the use of following example:--

If the true value for a result is 2.00g and a student 'A' takes two measurements and reports the results as 1.95g and 1.93g. then these values are found precise as they are close to each other but are not accurate.

Another student 'B' repeats the experiment and obtains 1.94g and 2.05g as the results for two measurements. These observations are neither precise nor accurate.

When a third student 'C' repeats these measurements and reports 2.01g and 1.99g as the result then these values are found precise as well as accurate.

Measurements /g			
	1	2	Average(g)
Student A	1.95	1.93	1.940
Student B	1.94	2.05	1.995
Student C	2.01	1.99	2.000

Data used to illustrate precision and accuracy

UNIT-II

(a) ACID BASE TITRATION

ACID BASE TITRATION:--Acid base titration is such type of titration which is used for the determination of strong acid, like hydrochloric acid by titrating with strong base like sodium hydroxide, weak acid like acetic acid with sodium hydroxide, weak base like ammonium hydroxide with hydrochloric acid and ammonium hydroxide with acetic acid respectively in the presence of suitable acid base indicators like methyl orange, phenolphthalein, bromophenol blue and mixture of neutral red and methylene blue indicators depending upon the nature of the reaction by getting colour changes at the end of the reaction.

Finally amount or strength of unknown substances is being determined by the help of consumed volume of titrant and I.P. factor by the use of proper calculation.

THEORY OF INDICATORS

Or,

THEORY OF NEUTRALIZATION INDICATORS:--

An amount of acid can be determined by titrating an alkaline solution with a standard solution of acid which is exactly equivalent chemically to the amount of base present. The point at which this is reached is the equivalence point or stoichiometric point or theoretical end point and results the formation of an aqueous solution of the corresponding salt.

If both the acid and base are strong electrolytes, the resultant solution will be neutral and have a pH of 7 but if either the acid or the base is a weak electrolyte, the salt will be hydrolysed to a certain degree and the solution at the equivalent point will be either slightly alkaline or slightly acid.

The exact pH of the solution at the equivalence point can readily be calculated from the ionsiation constant of the weak acid or the weak base and the concentration of the solution.

For any actual titration the correct end point will be characterized by a definite value of the hydrogen-ion concentration of the solution, the value depending upon the nature of the acid and the base and the concentration of the solution.

Neutralization or acid-base indicators are such type of substances which possess different colours according to the hydrogen ion concentration of the solution.

The chief characteristic of acid-base indicators is that the change from a predominantly 'acid' colour to a predominantly 'alkaline' colour, is not sudden and abrupt, but takes place within a small interval of pH (usually about two pH units) termed the colour-change interval of the indicator.

The position of the colour-change interval in the pH scale varies widely with different indicators.

Theory of indicator or acid-base indicator or neutralization indicator can be explained on the basis of following two principles:--

(1) OSTWALD THEORY OF INDICATOR:--

As per this theory all indicators are very weak organic acids or bases.

Ostwald considered that the undissociated indicator acid (HIn) or base (InOH) had a different colour from that of its ion.

The equilibria in aqueous solution can be written as such:--

HIn $\rightleftharpoons$ H$^+$ + In$^-$

and

InOH $\rightleftharpoons$ In$^+$ + OH$^-$

Unionised Ionised

colour colour

If the indicator is a free amine or substituted amine, then equilibrium is as such:--

In + H$_2$O $\rightleftharpoons$ OH$^-$ + HIn$^+$

Let us consider an indicator which is a weak acid.

In acid solution ie., in the presence of excess of H$^+$ ions, the ionization will be dispersed (common-ion effect) and the concentration of In$^-$ will be very small, the colour will be that of the unionized form.

If medium is alkaline, then the decrease of [H$^+$] will be result in the further ionization of the indicator[In-] increases and the colour of the ionized form becomes apparent.

By applying law of mass action,

we obtain,

$$\frac{a_{H^+} \times a_{In^-}}{a_{HIn}} = \frac{[H^+][In^-]}{HIn} \times \frac{YH^+ \times Yn^-}{Y_{HIn}} = K_{in}$$

and

$$[H^+] = \frac{[HIn]}{[In^-]} \times K_{in} \times \frac{YHIn}{YH^+ . YIn^-} = \frac{[Un-ionised\ form]}{[Ionised\ form]} \times K_{in} \times \frac{YHIn}{YH^+ . YIn^-}$$

where,

Kin = ionization constant of the indicator.

If the activity coefficients are assumed to be unity then above equation reduces to the simplified concentration form :

$$[H^+] = \frac{[HIn]}{[In^-]} \times K_{in} = \frac{[Un-ionised\ form]}{[Ionised\ form]} \times K_{in}$$

The actual colour of the indicator which depends upon the ratio of the concentrations of the ionized and un-ionised forms, is thus directly related to the hydrogen-ion concentration.

Above equation can be written logarithmically

$$pH = \log \frac{[In^-]}{[HIn]} + pK_{in}$$

For an indicator which is a weak base an exactly analogous expression to above equation can be deduced which in its simplified form is

$$[OH^-] = \frac{[InOH]}{[In^+]} \times K_{in}$$

where K_{in} = corresponding base dissociation constant.

This may be written:--

$$[H^+] = \frac{K_w \times [In^+]}{K_{in} \times [InOH]}$$

where $K_w = [H^+] \times [OH^-]$ (approximately)

(2)

TRANSFORMATION OF BENZENOID TO QUINONOID STRUCTURE AND IN VICE VERSA:--

Theory of indicator also can be explained on the basis of transformation of benzenoid structure to quinonoid structure or vice versa with changes in the hydrogen ion concentration.

As per earlier theories of Bernthsen, Friedlander and Witt, colour in organic compounds is associated with the presence of certain unsaturated chromophores such as C = C, C = O, N = O and N = N especially when intensified by 'auxochromes' such as NH_2 and OH.

Further importance of the p-quionoid chromophoric system had been recognized and it became clear that the colour changes of many indicators can be explained on the basis of transformation of a benzenoid structure into a quinonoid structure or vice versa, with changes in the hydrogen ion concentration of the solution.

Benzenoid form
(colourless)

Quinonoid form
(coloured)

Later nature of this change was demonstrated by Armstrong in case of nitrophenols.

(I) p-nitrophenol is present as yellow ion in alkaline solution while in acid solutions, it is present as nearly colourless nitro-compound.

OH—⟨C$_6$H$_4$⟩—NO$_2$ ⇌ O=⟨C$_6$H$_4$⟩=NO$_2^-$

Almost colourless   Deep yellow

(II) Phenolphthalein indicator is colourless in acid or neutral solution which becomes red in slightly alkaline solution and red colour fades in strongly alkaline solution. Such colour changes are due to changes in structure in the presence of different medium.

Lactone, colourless in acid solution ⇌ Quinonoid salt, red in alkaline solution

⇌ [Phenolic salt of carbinol structure]

Phenolic salt, of carbinol, colourless in strong alkaline solution

(III) Methyl orange indicator is yellow in alkaline solution due to $-N=N-$ group and it changes into red quinonoid form in presence of acid solution.

[Methyl orange alkaline form structure] ⇌ [Quinonoid form structure]

Methyl orange alkaline form, yellow in neutral or alkaline solution

Quinonoid form red in acid solution

CLASSIFICATION OF ACID BASE TITRATIONS AND THEORY INVOLVED IN TITRATIONS OF STRONG, WEAK AND VERY WEAK ACIDS AND BASES:--

Acid base titration can be classified as such:--

(1) Titration of a strong acid with a strong base

(2) Titration of a weak acid with a strong base

(3) Titration of a weak base with a strong acid

(4) Titration of a weak acid with a weak base

(1) TITRATION OF A STRONG ACID WITH A STRONG BASE:--

Let us consider titration of a 100ml. of strong acid like M-HCl acid with a 100ml. of strong base like M-NaOH solution.

During the process of titration both are completely dissociated. So activity coefficients of the ions can be taken as unity in order to calculate the change of pH during the process of neutralization of strong acid with strong base.

The pH of M-HCl acid is 0.

When 50ml. of the M base is being added then 50ml. of un-neutralised M acid will be present in a total volume of 150ml.

So, $[H^+]$ will be $50 \times \frac{1}{150} = 3.33 \times 10^{-3}$

$$or,$$
$$pH = 0.48$$

For 75ml. of base, $[H^+] = 25 \times \frac{1}{175} = 1.43 \times 10^{-1}, pH = 0.84$

For 90ml. of base, $[H^+] = 10 \times \frac{1}{190} = 5.26 \times 10^{-2}, pH = 1.3$

For 98ml. of base, $[H^+] = 2 \times \frac{1}{198} = 1.01 \times 10^{-2}, pH = 2.0$

For 99 ml. of base, $[H^+] = 1 \times \frac{1}{199} = 5.03 \times 10^{-3}, pH = 2.3$

For 99.9 ml. of base, $[H^+] = 01 \times \frac{1}{199.9} = 5.00 \times 10^{-4}, pH = 3.3$

Upon the addition of 100ml. of the base, the pH changes sharply to 7,

i.e., the theoretical equivalence point provided carbon dioxide is absent.

With 100.1ml. of base,

$[OH^-] = 0.1/200.1$

= 5.00 x 10^{-4}

pOH = 3.3 and pH = 10.7

with 101ml. of base,

[OH-] = 1/201 = 5.0x 10^{-3}

Hence, pOH = 2.3 and pH = 11.7

Now, it is clear that when titration proceeds, initially the pH rises slowly but between the addition of 99.9 and 100.1 ml.of alkali, the pH of the solution rises from 3.3 to 10.7 i.e., in the vicinity of the equivalence point the rate of change of pH of the solution is very rapid.

The complete results can be extended to 200ml. of alkali as shown in Table-1 and it also includes the figures for 0.1M and 0.01M solutions of acid and base respectively. The additions of alkali have been extended in all three cases to 200ml. The data in the table -1 also can be represented graphically in Fig-1.

Table – 1: pH during titration of 100 cm³ of HCl with NaOH of equal concentration.

Cm³ of NaOH added	M solution pH	0.1 M solution pH	0.01 M solution pH
0	0.0	1.0	2.0
50	0.5	1.5	2.5
75	0.8	1.8	2.8
90	1.3	2.3	3.3
98	2.0	3.0	4.0
99	2.3	3.3	4.3
99.5	2.6	3.6	4.6
99.8	3.0	4.0	5.0
99.9	3.3	4.3	5.3
100.0	7.0	7.0	7.0
100.1	10.7	9.7	8.7
100.2	11.0	10.0	9.0
100.5	11.4	10.4	9.4
101	11.7	10.7	9.7
102	12.0	11.0	10.0
110	12.7	11.7	10.7
125	13.0	12.0	11.0
150	13.3	12.3	11.3
200	13.5	12.5	11.5

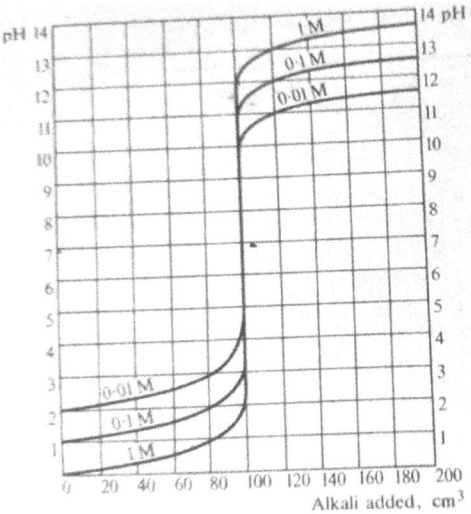

Fig-1:- Neutralization curves of 100 cm³ of HCl with NaOH of same concentration

With M solutions:--

It is evident that any acid base indicator with an effective range between pH 3 and 10.5 can be used. The colour change is observed as sharp and titration error is found negligible.

With 0.1M solution:--

The ideal pH range for an indicator is limited to 4.5-9.5. When 99.8 ml. of alkali is added, then methyl orange exists chiefly in the alkaline form and titration error is found about 0.2 % which is negligibly small for most practical purposes. The titration error is also negligibly small with phenolphthalein.

With 0.01M solutions:--

Methyl red, bromothymol blue or phenol red are found suitable for ideal pH range of 5.5-8.5. The titration error in case of methyl orange is 1-2 percent.

(2) TITRATION OF A WEAK ACID WITH A STRONG BASE:--

Let us consider titration of 100ml. of 0.1M acetic acid with 100 ml of 0.1M sodium hydroxide solution. The pH of the solution at the equivalence point can be given as such:-

pH = ½ pkw + ½ pKa − ½ pc

where pKw = logarithm (to the base 10) of the reciprocal of the ionization constant of water.

pKa = logarithm of the reciprocal of the dissociation constant of acid

pc = logarithm of the reciprocal of the concentration of salt i.e., NaCl

= 7 + 2.37 − ½ (1.3)

= 8.72

For the concentrations, approximate mass action expression can be employed as such:--

$$[H^+] \times \frac{[CH_3COO^-]}{[CH_3COOH]} = Ka : ---\text{I}$$

Or, $[H^+] = [CH_3COOH] \times Ka/[CH_3COO^-]$

Or, $pH = Log \frac{[Salt]}{[Acid]} + pKa$

The concentration of the salt (and of the acid) at any point can be calculated from the volume of alkali added.

The initial pH of 0.1M acetic acid is computed from equation (I); the dissociation of the acid is relatively so small that it may be neglected in expressing the concentration of acetic acid.

Hence, from equation (I);

$$[H^+] \times [CH_3COO^-]/[CH_3COOH] = 1.82 \times 10^{-5}$$

Or, $[H^+]2/0.1 = 1.82 \times 10^{-5}$

Or, $[H^+] = \sqrt{1.82 \times 10^{-6}} = 1.35 \times 10^{-3}$

Or,

pH = 2.87

When 50ml. of 0.1M-alkali has been added

then,

$$[salt] = 50 \times 0.1 \times 150 = 3.33 \times 10^{-2}$$

and

$$[acid] = 50 \times \frac{0.1}{150} = 3.33 \times 10^{-2}$$

$pH = log(3.33 \times 10^{-2}/3.33 \times 10^{-2}) + 4.74$

= 4.74

The pH values at other points on the titration curve can be calculated similarly.

After the equivalence point solution contains excess of OH⁻ ions which represents the hydrolysis of salt; the pH may be assumed with sufficientaccuracy.

All the result collected in Table 2 and are depicted graphically in Fig2.

Table 2 : Neutralization of 100 cm² of 0.1 M- acetic acid ($K_a = 1.82 \times 10^{-5}$) and of 100 cm² of 0.1 M-HA ($K_a = 1 \times 10^{-7}$) with 0.1 M sodium hydroxide

Cm³ of 0.1 M-NaOH Used	0.1 M acetic acid pH	0.1 M- HA ($K_a=1\times10^{-7}$) pH
0	2.9	4.0
10	3.8	6.0
25	4.3	6.5
50	4.7	7.0
90	5.7	8.0
99.0	6.7	9.0
99.5	7.0	9.3
99.8	7.4	9.7
99.9	7.7	9.8
100.0	8.7	9.9
100.2	10.0	10.0
100.5	10.4	10.4
101	10.7	10.7
110	11.7	11.7
125	12.0	12.0
150	12.3	12.3
200	12.5	12.5

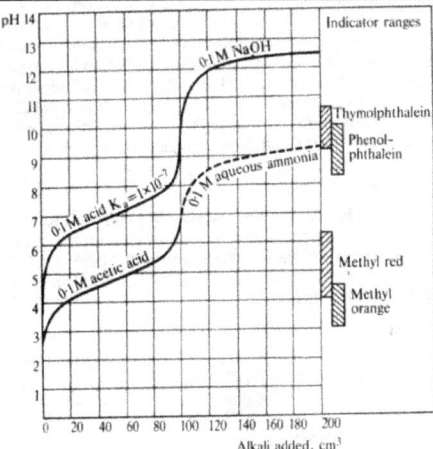

Fig-2 : Neutralization curve of 0.1 M-acetic acid and of 0.1M-acid ($K_a = 1\times10^{-7}$) with 0.1 M-sodium hydroxide (calculated)

The results for the titration of 100ml. of 0.1M solution of a weaker acid (Ka = 1 x 10⁻⁷) with 0.1M sodium hydroxide at the laboratory temperature are also included.

For 0.1M acetic acid and 0.1M sodium hydroxide, it is evident from the titration curve that neither methyl orange nor methyl red can be used as indicator.

The equivalence point is at pH 8.7 and it is necessary to use an indicator with a pH range on the slightly alkaline side, such as phenolphthalein, thymolphthalein or thymol blue (pH range, as base, 8.0-9.6)

With thymolphthalein, colour change covers the pH range 9.3-10.5.

End point is obtained as more sharp in compare of thymolphthalein than phenolphthalein.

In general, weak acids ($Ka > 5 \times 10^{-6}$) can be titrated with thymolphthalein, phenolphthalein or thymol blue as indicators.

(3) TITRATION OF A WEAK BASE WITH A STRONG ACID:--

Let us study the titration of 100ml. of 0.1M aqueous ammonia ($Kb = 1.8 \times 10^{-5}$) with 0.1M HCl acid at the ordinary laboratory temperature.

The pH of the solution at the equivalence point can be given as such:--

pH = ½ pKw – ½ pKb + ½ pc

where,

pKb = logarithm of the reciprocal of the dissociation constant of the acid

= 7 – 2.37 + ½ (1.3)

= 5.28

pH can be calculated with sufficient accuracy for other concentration as such:--

$$[NH_4^+] \times \frac{[OH^-]}{[NH_3]} = Kb$$

Or,

$$[OH^-] = [NH_3] \times Kb/[NH_4^+]$$

Or,

pOH = log [salt]/[base] + pKb

Or,

pH = pKw – pKb – log [salt/[base]

After the equivalence point solution contains excess of H$^+$ ions and hydrolysis of salt gets repressed.

The results computed in the above manner can be represented graphically in Fig.3 The results for the titration of 100ml. of a 0.1M solution of a weaker base ($Kb = 1 \times 10^{-7}$) are also included.

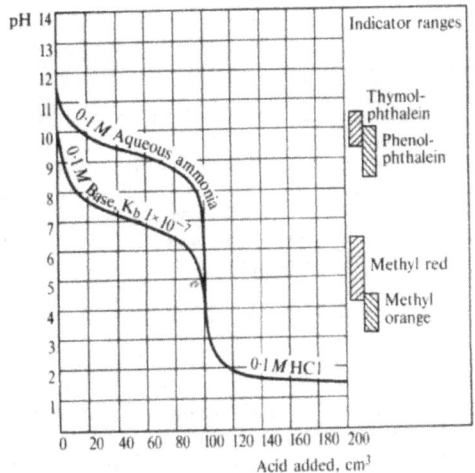

Fig – 3: Neutralization curves of 100 cm³ of 0.1 M- aqueous ammonia (K_a =1.8x10⁻⁵) and of M-base (K_b = 1 x 10⁻⁷) with 0.1 M-Hydrochloric acid

Now it is clear that neither thymolphthalein nor phenolphthalein can be used in the titration of 0.1M aqueous ammonia. The equivalence point is at pH 5.3.

It is necessary to use an indicator with a pH range on the slightly acid side (3 – 6.5) such as methylorange, methyl red, bromophenol blue or bromocresol green.

Bromo-phenol blue or methyl orange can be used for weak base (K_b = 1x10⁻⁷).

No sharp colour change is obtained with bromo-cresol green or with methyl red and the titration error will be considerable.

(4) TITRATION OF A WEAK ACID WITH A WEAK BASE:--

Let us discuss the titration of 100ml. of 0.1M acetic acid (K_a = 1.8 x 10⁻⁵) with 0.1M – aqueous ammonia (K_b = 1.8 x 10⁻⁵).

The pH of the equivalence point can be given as such:--

pH = ½ pKw + ½ pKa – ½ pKb

= 7.0 + 2.37 – 2.37

= 7.0

The titration curve for the neutralization of 100ml. of 0.1M acetic acid with 100 ml of 0.1M aqueous ammonia at the laboratory temperature is shown by the dotted line in Fig 2.

The chief feature of the curve is that the change of pH near the equivalence point and during the whole of the neutralization curve is very gradual.

There is no sudden change in pH and hence no sharp end point can be found with any simple indicator.

A mixed indicator, which exhibits a sharp colour change over a very limited pH range, is found suitable.

For example, a mixed indicator like neutral red and methyene blue indicator can be used for titration of acetic acid-ammonia solutions.

NEUTRALIZATION CURVES:--

Concept of neutralization process is obtained by studying the charges in [H^+] ion concentration during the course of appropriate titration.

The change in pH near to equivalence point is of great importance which helps us to select an indicator which will give the smallest titration error.

The curve obtained by plotting pH as ordinates against the percentage of acid neutralized (or number of cm^3 of alkali added) as abscissa is known as neutralization or titration cruve.

This can be determined experimentally by finding of pH at various stages during the titration of a potentiometric method.

e.g.;

Let us consider neutralization of a strong acid and a strong base.

Let us study a titration between 1M of HCl acid and 1M of NaOH.

The pH of 1M HCl = 0

When 50ml. of 1M NaOH is added then 50ml. of unneutralised 1M HCl will be present in a total volume of 150 ml.

[H+] = 50x1/150 = 3.33 x 10^{-1} or pH = 0.48

For 75 ml. of base, [H^+] = 25 x 1/175 = 1.43 x 10^{-1}, pH = 0.84

For 99 ml. of base, [H^+] = 1 x 1/199 = 5 x 0.03 x 10^{-3}, pH = 2.3

Upon addition of 100ml of base, the pH will change sharply to 7.

A graph can be obtained to get neutralization curve in between the titration of 100ml. of HCl with NaOH of same concentration in following manner:--

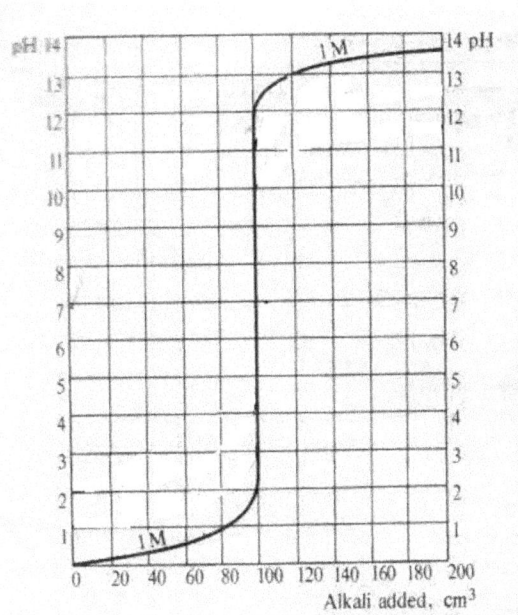

Fig.4:-- Neutralisation curve of 100 ml of 1 M HCl with 100 ml of 1 M NaOH

(b) NON AQUEOUS TITRATION:-

Non aqueous titration is also known as acid-base titrations in non aqueous solvents.

NON AQUEOUS SOLVENTS:--

Non aqueous solvents are such type of solvents which should be free from water or they should be anhydrous in nature. They are involved in the transfer of protons when an acid reacts with a base or in viceversa.

TYPES OF NON AQUEOUS SOLVENTS:--

Non aqueous solvents are of four types:--

1) AMPHIPROTIC SOLVENTS:--

Amphiprotic solvents are such type of solvents which can accept or donate protons and can behave as acids or bases. They produce levelling effect by masking the relative strengths of acids or bases.

Examples:--

Water, alcohol and acetic acid.

(2) BASIC OR PROTOPHILLIC SOLVENTS:--

Basic or protophillic solvents are such type of solvents which can accept protons.

Examples:--

Acetone, ethers (including dioxan) and amines eg. formdimethylamide and pyridine

(3) ACIDIC SOLVENTS:--

Acidic solvents are such type of solvents which can donate protons.

Examples:--

Pure sulphuric acid, hydrogen fluoride

(4) APROTIC(OR INERT) SOLVENTS:--

Aprotic solvents are such type of solvents which neither accept nor donate protons.

Examples:--

Chloroform, benzene.

They do not exert levelling effect.

THEORY OR PRINCIPLE OF NON AQUEOUS TITRATION:--

Non aqueous titration is such type of titration which is used for the determination of weak bases like salt of aliphatic or aromatic carboxylic acids eg. Sodium acetate, sodium benzoate, too weakly basic substances like ephedrine hydrochloride, very weak acids like barbiturates, chlorthiazide, diloxanide furoate, bendrofluazide, hydrochlorothiazide and hydroflumethiazide, by titrating with standard solution of suitable titrants like perchloric acid, sodium methoxide, lithium methoxide, tetra butyl ammonium hydroxide in thepresence of non aqueous solvents like acetic acid, dioxan, dimethylformamide solution, pyrimidine and suitable indicators like crystal violet, thymol blue, quinaldine red, 1-naphthol benzein solution.

Theory of non-aqueous titration can be explained by taking example of titration of weak base like sodium acetate with standard solution of 0.1M perchloric acid in the presence of anhydrous acetic acid solvent and 1-naphthol benzein solution indicator.

During the process of the titration at first sodium acetate ionizes into sodium ion and acetate ion. Further perchloric acid reacts with anhydrous glacial acetic acid and produces protonated acetic acid and perchlorate ion. Finally acetate ion combines with protonated acetic acid and forms two moles of acetic acid. End point is obtained as blue to green colour.

REACTION:--

$$CH_3CONa \longrightarrow CH_3COO^- + Na^+$$

$$HClO_4 + CH_3COOH \longrightarrow CH_3COOH_2^+ + ClO_4^-$$

$$CH_3COOH_2^+ + CH_3COO^- \longrightarrow 2CH_3COOH$$

METHOD:--

About 0.25g of sodium acetate is dissolved in 50ml. of anhydrous glacial acetic acid. Then 5ml. of acetic anhydrdide is added. It is mixed and allowed to stand for 30 minutes.

After that 0.3ml. of 1-naptholbenzein solution is added as indicator. Further it is titrated with standard solution of 0.1M perchloric acid until a green colour is obtained.

A blank determination is performed and made any necessary correction.

Each ml. of 0.1M perchloric acid is equivalent to 0.00820g of $C_2H_3NaO_2$.

PREPARATION OF 0.1M PERCHLORIC ACID:--

750ml. of glacial acetic acid is cooled to about 15°C.

Then 11.0ml. of Perchloric acid is added to this with continuous stirring by adding 1ml. at a time so that the temperature does not rise. Mixture is cooled to 10°C but without freezing it.

Then sufficient amount of acetic anhydride (calculated to combine with water in the perchloric acid) is added dropwise from a burette in such a way that temperature should not rise more than 0.5°C.

Further temperature is allowed to rise to 15°C. Then volume is made up to 1.0 litre by the use of glacial acetic acid at 20°C with sufficient stirring.

STANDARDIZATION OF 0.1M PERCHLORIC ACID:--

METHOD:--

(1) About 50ml. of 0.1N sodium acetate (13.61g in 1 liter of water) is taken in a conical flask and made water free by the use of acetic anhydride. Then 1.0ml. of solution of α - naptholbenzein is added as indicator and titrated with 0.1N perchloric acid by getting emerald green colour at end point.

Then exact normality is determined by using $N_1V_1 = N_2V_2$ formula where N_1 and N_2 = normality of perchloric acid and sodium acetate where as V_1 and V_2 are consumed volume of perchloric acid and taken volume of sodium acetate.

(2) 0.5g of potassium hydrogen phthalate, C_6H_4 (COOK)COOH (Previously dried at 120°C for 2 hours) is dissolved in 50ml. of anhydrous glacial acetic acid in a conical falsk. Then 2 drops of crystal violet indicator is added and titrated with 0.1N perchloric acid by getting emerald green colour as end point.

$$Normality\ of\ perchloric\ acid = \frac{Weight\ of\ potassium\ hydrogen\ phthalate}{Consumed\ volume\ of\ 0.1N\ perchloric\ acid\ \times 0.2042}$$

TYPES OF NON AQUEOUS TITRATION

Or,

APPLICATIONS OF NON AQUEOUS TITRATION

Or,

DETERMINATION OF NON AQUEOUS TITRATION:--

There are four applications or types of non aqueous titration:--

(1) TITRATION OF WEAK BASES:--

Non aqueous titration is used for the determination of weak bases like sodium acetate.

It is already discussed under the theory or principle of nonaqueous titration.

(2) TITRATION OF TOO WEAK BASES:--

PRINCIPLE:--

Non aqueous titration is used for the determination of too weak bases like ephedrine hydrochloride. During the process of determination, ephedrine hydrochloride ionizes into halide ion i.e, Cl^-. Chloride ion is too weakly basic and it reacts with perchloric acid in presence of acetic acid. Addition of mercuric acetate replaces the halide ion by an equivalent quantity of acetate ion which is a strong base in acetic acid.

Further acetate ion combines with protonated acetic acid which is obtained when perchloric acid combines with acetic acid.

$$2C_{10}H_{15}NO, HCl \rightleftharpoons C_{10}H_{16}N^+O + 2Cl^-$$

Ephedrine hydrochloride (weak base)   (too weakly basic)

$(CH_3COO)_2Hg$ (undissociated) + $2Cl^- \rightleftharpoons HgCl_2$ (undissociated) + $2CH_3COO^-$ (strong base)

$$HClO_4 + CH_3COOH \rightleftharpoons CH_3COOH_2^+ + ClO_4^-$$

$$2CH_3COO^- + 2CH_3COOH_2^+ \rightleftharpoons 4CH_3COOH$$

Ephedrine hydrochloride is estimated with standard solution of 0.1N perchloric acid in the presence of anhydrous acetic acid and mercuric acetate by the use of crystal violet as indicator. At the end point a blue green colour is obtained.

METHOD:--

0.15g of ephedrine hydrochloride is taken in a conical flask. 30ml. of anhydrous glacial acetic acid and 10ml. of mercuric acetate solution are added. It is warmed gently to effect solution, cooled and titrated with 0.1Mperchloric acid solution by using 0.1ml.of crystal violet solution as indicator. At the end point a green blue colour is obtained.

A blank determination is performed and made any necessary correction.

Each ml. of 0.1M perchloric acid is equivalent to 0.02017g of $C_{10}H_{15}NO, HCl$.

(3) TITRATION OF VERY WEAK ACIDS:--

(i) Estimation of barbiturates:--

PRINCIPLE:--

Non aqueous titration is used for determination of very weak acids like such as compounds exhibiting lactam-lactim tautomerism barbiturates by using metallic oxides like standard sodium methoxide solution as titrant in the presence of protophillic solvent like dimethyl formamide non aqueous solvent and thymol blue as indicator or in pyridine solution.

Barbiturate exhibits lactam-lactim tautomerism.

$$OC \underset{NH-CO}{\overset{NH-CO}{<}} CRR^I$$

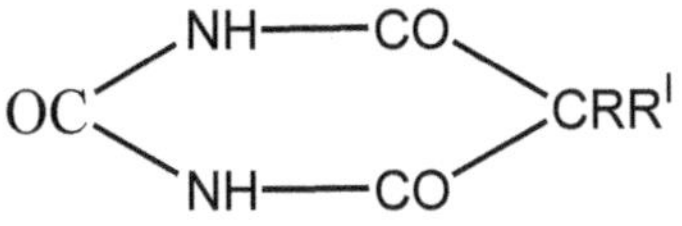

Barbiturate

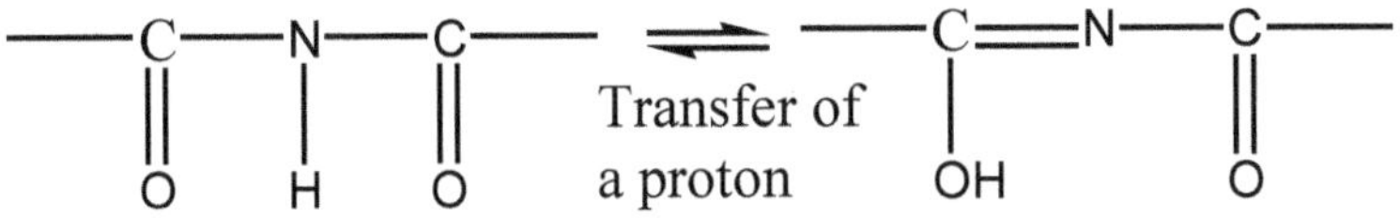

Lactam form ⇌ (Transfer of a proton) Lactim form

REACTIONS:--

$$-NH-CO \rightleftharpoons -N=C(OH)-$$

$$-N=C(O^-H^+) + (CH_3)_2NCOH \longrightarrow (CH_3)_2NCOH_2^+ + -N=C(O^-)$$

or S   or SH^+ (Where S = solvent)

or

$$-N=C(O^-)- + Na^+OMe^- \longrightarrow -N=C(O^-Na^+)- + MeO^- \text{ or } CH_3O^-$$

$$(CH_3)_2NCOH_2^+ + CH_3O^- \longrightarrow CH_3OH + (CH_3)_2NCOH$$

Net result is,

$$-N=C(OH) + NaOMe \longrightarrow -N=C(ONa) + MeOH$$

Non aqueous titration can be used for the determination of barbiturate by titrating with standard solution of Lithium methoxide in the presence of quinaldine red as indicator..

—N═══C(OH) + LiOMe ⟶ —N═══C(OLi)— + MeOH

PREPARATION OF 0.1M SODIUM METHOXIDE:--

150ml. of anhydrous methanol is cooled in ice water and 2.5g of freshly cut sodium is added in small protions. When the metal has dissolved then sufficient toluene previously dried over sodium wire is added to produce 1000ml.

STANDARDISATION OF 0.1M SODIUM METHOXIDE:--

Sodium methoxide can be standardized with benzoic acid solution in the presence of dimethylformamide solvent and thymolphthalein indicator. At endpoint a blue colour is obtained.

$$CH_3ONa + C_6H_5COOH \longrightarrow C_6H_5COONa + CH_3OH$$

METHOD:--

0.4g of benzoic acid is dissolved in 80ml. of dimethylformamide. 0.15ml. of thymolphthalein solution is added and titrated with the sodium methoxide solution to a blue end point.

The solution is protected from atmoshpheric carbon dioxide throughout the titration.

A blank determination is performed and made any necessary correction.

Each ml of 0.1M sodium methoxide is equivalent to 0.01221g of $C_7H_6O_2$

(ii) ESTIMATION OF CHLORTHIAZIDE:--

Non aqueous titration is also used for determination of chlorthiazide by titrating with standard solution of 0.1N Lithium methoxide in presence of bromothymol blue as indicator.

(4) TITRATION OF WEAKER ACIDS:--

Non aqueous titration can be used for determination of weaker acids like diloxanide furoate, bendrofluazide, hydrochlorthiazide and hydroflumethiazide by titrating with quaternary ammonium hydroxide titrant like tetrabutyl ammonium hydroxide, $N(C_4H_9)_4^+OH^-$ in the presence of anhydrous pyridine potentiometrically.

Example:--

Estimation of hydrochlorthiazide;

or $C_7H_8ClN_3O_4S_2$

METHOD:--

About 0.12g of hydrochlorthiazide is dissolved in 50ml. of anhydrous pyridine and titrated with 0.1M tetrabutylammonium hydroxide titrant potentiometrically. A blank determination is performed and any necessary correction is made.

Each ml. of 0.1M tetrabutylammonium hydroxide is equivalent to 0.01488g of $C_7H_8ClN_3O_4S_2$.

PREPARATION OF 0.1M TETRABUTYLAMMONIUM HYDROXIDE:--

40g of tetrabutylammonium iodide is dissolved in 90ml. of dehydrated methanol in a glass- stoppered flask.It is placed in an ice bath. 20g of powdered silver oxide is added. The stopper is inserted and agitated vigorously for 1 hour.A few ml. is centrifuged and supernatant liquid is tested for iodides by treating with silver nitrate solution in the presence of dilute nitric acid. A curdy yellow precipitate confirms the presence of iodides. If the test is positive, then an additional 2g of silver oxide is added and continued to stand for 30 minutes with intermittent agitation.

When all the iodide has reacted, then it is filtered through sintered glass filter. The flask is rinsed and filtered with three quantities, each of 50ml., of anhydrous toluene.

Washing is added to the filtrate and diluted to 1000ml. with anhydrous toluene. The solution is flushed for 10 minutes with dry, carbondioxide-free nitrogen. It is stored in a container protected from carbon dioxide and moisture and after 60 days it is discarded.

STANDARDIZATION OF 0.1MTETRABUTYLAMMONIUM HYDROXIDE:--

About 0.4g of benzoic acid is dissolved in 80ml. of dimethylformamide. A few drops of a 1.0% w/v solution of thymol blue indicator in dimethylformamide are added and titrated with the tetrabutylammonium hydroxide solution to a blue end point.The solution is protected from atmospheric carbon dioxide throughout the titration.

A blank determination is performed and made any necessary correction.

Each ml. of 0.1M tetrabutylammonium hydroxide is equivalent to 0.01221g of $C_7H_6O_2$

ESTIMATION OF SODIUM BENZOATE:--

PRINCIPLE:--

Sodium benzoate can be estimated with standard solution of 0.1M perchloric acid in the presence of anhydrous acetic acid solvent and 1-naphthol benzein solution indicator.

During the process of titration at first sodium benzoate ionizes into sodium ion and benzoate ion. Then perchloric acid combines with anhydrous glacial acetic acid and produces protonated acetic acid and perchlorate ion.

Finally benzoate ion combines with protonated acetic acid and forms one mole of acetic acid and one mole of benzoic acid. End point is obtained as blue to green colour.

$C_6H_5COONa \rightleftharpoons C_6H_5COO^- + Na^+$

$$HClO_4 + CH_3COOH \rightleftharpoons CH_3COOH_2^+ + ClO_4^-$$

$$C_6H_5COO^- + CH_3COOH_2^+ \rightleftharpoons CH_3COOH + C_6H_5COOH$$

METHOD:--

About 0.25g of sodium benzoate is dissolved in 20ml. of anhydrous glacial acetic acid. Then 5ml. of acetic anhydride is added. It is mixed and allowed to stand for 30 minutes.

Then 0.05ml. of 1-naphtholbenzein solution is added as indicator. Further it is titrated with standard solution of 0.1M perchloric acid until a green colour is obtained.

A blank determination is performed and made any necessary correction.

ESTIMATION OF EPHEDRINE HYDROCHLORIDE:--

PRINCIPLE:--

Ephedrine hydrochloride can be estimated by the use of non aqueous titration method by using 0.1 N perchloric acid as titrant and crystal violet as indicator in the presence of anhydrous acetic acid as solvent. At the end point a blue green colour is obtained.

During the process of determination, ephedrine hydrochloride ionizes into halide ion i.e, Cl^-. Chloride ion is too weakly basic and it reacts with perchloric acid in presence of acetic acid. Addition of mercuric acetate replaces the halide ion by an equivalent quantity of acetate ion which is a strong base in acetic acid.

Further acetate ion combines with protonated acetic acid which is obtained when perchloric acid combines with acetic acid.

$$2C_{10}H_{15}NO, HCl \rightleftharpoons C_{10}H_{16}N^+O + 2Cl^-$$

Ephedrine hydrochloride (weak base)   (too weakly basic)

$$(CH_3COO)_2Hg \text{ (undissociated)} + 2Cl^- \rightleftharpoons HgCl_2 \text{ (undissociated)} + 2CH_3COO^- \text{(strong base)}$$

$$HClO_4 + CH_3COOH \rightleftharpoons CH_3COOH_2^+ + ClO_4^-$$

$$2CH_3COO^- + 2CH_3COOH_2^+ \rightleftharpoons 4CH_3COOH$$

METHOD:--

0.15g of ephedrine hydrochloride is taken in a conical flask. 30ml. of anhydrous glacial acetic acid and 10ml. of mercuric acetate solution are added. It is warmed gently to effect solution, cooled and titrated with 0.1M perchloric acid solution by using 0.1ml.of crystal violet solution as indicator. At the end point a green blue colour is obtained.

A blank determination is performed and made any necessary correction.

Each ml. of 0.1M perchloric acid is equivalent to 0.02017g of $C_{10}H_{15}NO$, HCl.

UNIT-III

(a) PRECIPITATION TITRATIONS:--

Precipitation reaction is such type of titrimetric analysis or volumetric analysis which depends upon the combination of ions to form a simple precipitate as in the titration of silver ions with a solution of a chloride.

$$Ag^+ + Cl^- \longrightarrow AgCl$$

or,

$$AgNO_3 + NaCl \longrightarrow AgCl + NaNO_3$$

THEORY OF PRECIPITATION TITRATIONS

Or,

THEORY OF PRECIPITATION REACTIONS:--

When precipitation reaction utilizes silver nitrate as the regent or titrant and used for the determination of halide salts in the presence of precipitation indicators then it is also known as argentimetric process or titration.

Theory of precipitation titration can be explained by taking example of titration of standard sodium chloride solution with standard solution of silver nitrate.

Let us consider the changes in ionic concentration which occur during the titration of 100ml. of 0.1M sodium chloride with 0.1M silver nitrate.

The solubility product of silver chloride at the laboratory temperature is 1.2×10^{-10}.

The initial concentration of chloride ions, [Cl⁻] is 0.1 mole per dm³,

Or,

pCl⁻ =1

When 50cm³ of 0.1M silver nitrate have been added,

then 50cm³ of 0.1M sodium chloride remain in a total volume of 150cm³

Thus, $[Cl^-] = 50 \times \frac{0.1}{150} = 3.33 \times 10^{-2}$

Or,

pCl⁻ = 1.48

With 90cm³ of silver nitrate solution

$$[Cl^-] = 10 \times \frac{0.1}{190} = 5.3 \times 10^{-3}$$

Or,

$pCl^- = 2.28$

Now, $aAg^+ \times aCl^- \approx [Ag^+] \times [Cl^-]$

$= 1.2 \times 10^{-10}$

$= K_{Sol}\, AgCl$

Or,

$pAg^+ + pCl^- = 9.92 = pAgCl$

In the last calculation,

$pCl^- = 1.48$

Hence, $pAg^+ = 9.92 - pCl^-$

Or,

$pAg^+ = 9.92 - 1.48$

Or,

$pAg^+ = 8.44$

Like this, various concentrations of chloride and silver ions can be computed up to the equivalence point.

At the equivalence point,

$$Ag^+ = Cl^- = \sqrt{K_{SolAgCl}}$$

Or,

$$pAg^+ = pCl^- = \frac{1}{2}pAgCl = \frac{9.92}{2} = 4.96$$

and a standard solution of silver chloride with no excess of silver or chloride ions is present.

With 100.1cm³ of silver nitrate solution,

$$[Ag^+] = 0.1 \times \frac{0.1}{200.1} = 5 \times 10^{-5}$$

Or,

$pAg^+ = 4.30$;

$pCl^- = pAgCl - pAg^+$

Or,

$pCl^- = 9.92 - 4.30 = 5.62$

These data are described in table-3.

Similar value can be obtained for titration of 100cm³ of 0.1M potassium iodide with 0.1M silver nitrate.

It has been seen that by inspecting the silver-ion exponents in the neighborhood of the equivalence point (say, between 99.8 and 100.2) that there is a marked change in the silver-ion concentration, although the change is more pronounced for silver iodide than for silver chloride, since the solubility product of silver chloride, is about 10^6 larger than the silver iodide.

This is shown more clearly in the titration curve as shown in Fig.5 which represents the changes of pAg^+ in the range between 10 percent before and 10 per cent after the equivalence point in the titration of 0.1M-chloride and 0.1M-iodide respectively with 0.1M-silver nitrate.

Table-3:--Titration of 100cm³ of 0.1M NaCl and 100cm³ of 0.1M KI respectively with 0.1M AgNO₃ (KsolAgCl = 1.2 x 10⁻¹⁰, Ksol AgCl = 1.7 x 10⁻¹⁰)

Cm³ of 0.1M AgNO₃	Titration of chloride		Titration of iodide	
	pCl⁻	pAg⁺	pI⁻	pAg⁺
50	1.5	8.4	1.5	14.3
90	2.3	7.6	2.3	13.5
99.8	4.0	5.9	4.0	11.8
100.0	5.0	5.0	7.9	7.9
100.1	5.6	4.3	11.5	4.3
100.2	5.9	4.0	11.8	4.0

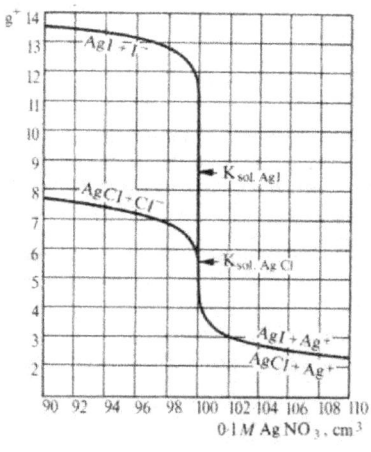

Fig-5:--Titration curves of 100 cm^3 of 0.1M NaCl and of 100 cm^3 of 0.1 M Kl respectively with 0.1M AgNO$_3$ (calculated)

TYPES OF PRECIPITATION TITRATIONS

Or,

TYPES OF PRECIPITATION REACTIONS

Or,

TYPES OF PRECIPITATION INDICATORS

Or,

DETERMINATION OF END-POINTS IN PRECIPITATION REACTIONS

Or,

END POINT DETECTION IN PRECIPITATION TITRATIONS:--

There are four types of precipitation titrations:--

(1) Formation of a coloured precipitate

Or,

Mohr's Method of precipitation titration

(2) Formation of a soluble coloured compound

Or,

Volhard's method of precipitation titration.

(3) Use of adsorption indicators

Or,

Fajans method of precipitation titration.

4)

Turbidity method

Or,

Gay-Lusac-Stas method

(1) FORMATION OF A COLOURED PRECIPITATE:--

Mohr's method is used for the determination of chloride and bromide.

Mohr's method of precipitation titration can be explained by taking example of titration of chloride ions with silver nitrate solution in the presence of neutral solution medium by using potassium chromate as indicator. At the end point chromate ions combine with silver ions to form the sparingly solube, red silver chromate precipitate.

$$Cl^- + Ag^+ \longrightarrow AgCl$$

$$CrO_4^= + 2Ag^+ \longrightarrow Ag_2CrO_4$$

$$NaCl + AgNO_3 \longrightarrow AgCl + NaNO_3$$

$$K_2CrO_4 + 2AgNO_3 \longrightarrow Ag_2CrO_4 + 2KNO_3$$

THEORY:--

Here a case of fractional precipitation of two sparingly soluble salts of silver chloride (K sol 1.2 x 10^{-10}) and silver chromate (K sol 1.7 x 10^{-12}) takes place.

Let us consider an example of titration of 0.1M sodium chloride with 0.1M silver nitrate in the presence of a few cm^3 of dilute potassium chromate solution indicator. Silver chloride is less soluble salt.

The initial chloride concentration is high hence silver chloride gets precipitated.

At the first point where red silver chromate is just precipitated, then both salts are found in equilibrium with the solution. Hence,

$$[Ag^+] \times [Cl^-] = KsolAgCl = 1.2 \times 10^{-10}$$

$$[Ag^+]^2 \times [CrO_4^{2-}] = Ksol\,Ag_2CrO_4 = 1.7 \times 10^{-12}$$

So,

$$[Ag^+] = \frac{KsolAgCl}{[Cl^-]} = \sqrt{\frac{KsolAg_2CrO_4}{[CrO_4^{2-}]}}$$

Or,

$$\frac{[Cl^-]}{\sqrt{CrO_4^{2-}}} = \frac{KsolAgCl}{\sqrt{KsolAg_2CrO_4}} = \frac{1.2 \times 10^{-10}}{\sqrt{1.7 \times 10^{-12}}} = 9.2 \times 10^{-5}$$

At the equivalence point,

$$[Cl^-] = \sqrt{KsolAgCl} = 1.1 \times 10^{-5}$$

If silver chromate gets precipitated at this chloride-ion concentration, then

$$[CrO_4^{2-}] = \left(\frac{Cl^-}{9.2 \times 10^{-5}}\right)^2 = \left(\frac{1.1 \times 10^{-5}}{9.2 \times 10^{-5}}\right)^2 = 1.4 \times 10^{-2}$$

Or,

potassium chromate concentration should be 0.014M.

It should be noted that a slight excess of silver nitrate solution should be added before the red colour of silver chromate is visible. It must be mentioned that the titration should be carried out in neutral solution or in very faintly alkaline solution within the pH range 6.5-9.0

In presence of acid solution, chromate ion concentration gets reduced and solubility product of silver chromate may not be exceeded because chromate ion produces dichromate ion in presence of acid solution.

$$2CrO_4^{2-} + 2H^+ \rightleftharpoons 2HCrO_4^- \rightleftharpoons Cr_2O_7^{2-} + H_2O$$

In presence of alkaline solution, silver hydroxide may get precipitated.

METHOD:--

About 25ml of 0.1M sodium chloride neutral solution is taken in conical flask and 1ml. of potassium chromate indicator solution is added. Then it is titrated with standard solution of 0.1M silver nitrate solution. At the end point a reddish-brown colour precipitate is obtained.

Each ml. of 0.1M silver nitrate is equivalent to 0.005844g of NaCl.

PREPARATION OF 0.1M AgNO3 SOLUTION:--

17.0 g of silver nitrate is dissolved in sufficient water to produce 1000ml.

STANDARDIZATION OF 0.1MSILVER NITRATE:--

0.1g of sodium chloride which is previously dried at 110°C for 2 hours, is dissolved in 5ml. of water. 5ml. of acetic acid, 50ml of methanol and 0.15ml. of eosin solution (adsorption indicator) are added and stirred preferably with magnetic stirrer. Then it is titrated with silver nitrate solution. At the end point a pink or red colour precipitate is formed.

Each ml. of 0.1M silver nitrate is equivalent to 0.005844g of NaCl.

(2) FORMATION OF A SOLUBLE COLOURED COMPOUND

Or,

VOLHARD'S METHOD OF PRECIPITATION TITRATION

Volhard's method is used for the titration of silver in the presence of free nitric acid with standard potassium or ammonium thiocyanate solution. Ferric nitrate or ferric ammonium sulphate solution is used as indicator.

At first thiocyanate solution produces a precipitate of silver thiocyanate.

$$Ag^+ + SCN^- \rightleftharpoons AgSCN$$

After the completion of this reaction, the slightest excess of thiocyanate solution produces a reddish-brown colouration due to formation of a complex ion.

$$Fe^{3+} + SCN^- \rightleftharpoons [Fe\,SCN]^{2+}$$

ii) Volhard's method is also applied for the determination of chlorides, bromides and iodides in acid solution.

Excess of standard silver nitrate solution is used and the excess is back titrated with standard thiocyanate solution.

(a) FOR THE CHLORIDE ESTIMATION:--

The following two equilibria are obtained during the titration of excess of silver ions,

$$Ag^+ + Cl^- \rightleftharpoons AgCl$$

$$Ag^+ + SCN^- \rightleftharpoons AgSCN$$

These two sparihgly soluble salts will be in equilibrium with the solution hence

$$\frac{[Cl^-]}{[SCN^-]} = \frac{KsolAgCl}{KsolAgSCN} = \frac{1.2 \times 10^{-10}}{7.1 \times 10^{-13}} = 169$$

When the excess of silver reacts then thiocyanate may also react with silver chloride since silver thiocyanate is less soluble salt than silver chloride

until the ratio $\frac{[Cl^-]}{[SCN^-]}$ in the solution is 169

$$AgCl + SCN^- \rightleftharpoons AgSCN + Cl^-$$

This reaction takes place before the occurring of the reaction in between Fe^{+++} and SCN^- in the solution.

So, it becomes necessary to prevent the reaction between the thiocyanate and silver chloride.

Prevention of reaction is done with the help of following methods:--

(i) The silver chloride should be filtered off before back titrating by boiling the suspension for few minutes by which most of the absorbed silver ions can be removed from its the surface of the precipitate before filtration. Further cold filtrate is titrated.

(ii) Potassium nitrate can be used as coagulant after the addition of silver nitrate for the purpose of prevention of adsorption of silver ions and further suspension is boiled for 3 minutes, cooled and titrated immediately.

(iii) Nitrobenzene can be used to coat the silver chloride particles by which interaction with thiocyanate can be prevented.

(b) FOR THE BROMIDE ESTIMATION:--

The following two equilibria during the titration of excess of silver ions, can be obtained.

$$\frac{[Br^-]}{[SCN^-]} = \frac{K_{sol}AgBr}{K_{sol}AgSCN} = \frac{3.5 \times 10^{-13}}{7.1 \times 10^{-13}} = 0.5$$

The titration error is found small and no difficulties are arised for the determination of end point.

c) For the iodide estimation, the titration error is found negligible as silver iodide is less soluble than bromide.

Iron (III) indicator should not be added until excess of silver is present since the dissolved iodide reacts with Fe^{3+} ions.

$$2Fe^{3+} + 2I^- \rightleftharpoons 2Fe^{2+} + I_2$$

PREPARATION OF 0.1M AMMONIUM THIOCYANATE:--

7.612g of ammonium thiocyanate is dissolved in sufficient water to produce 1000ml.

STANDARDIATION OF 0.1M AMMONIUM THIOCYANATE:--

30ml. of 0.1M silver nitrate into a glass-stoppered flask. Then it is diluted with 50ml. of water. 2ml. of nitric acid and 2ml. of ferric ammonium sulphate solution are added and titrated with the ammonium thiocyanate solution to the first appearance of a red-brown colour.

Each ml. of 0.1M silver nitrate is equivalent to 0.007612g of NH_4SCN.

(3) USE OF ADSORPTION INDICATORS

Or,

FAJANS METHOD OF PRECIPITATION TITRATION:--

Fajans method of precipitation titration is based on the nature of adsorption of adsorption indicator.

The action of adsorption indicator is due to fact that at the equivalence point the indicator is adsorbed by the precipitate and during the process of adsorption a change occurs in the indicator which leads to a substance of different colour, so they have been termed as adsorption indicators.

Adsorption indicator is used in the two form of dyes:--

(i) Acid dyes of fluorescein series eg. Fluorescein and eosin which are applied as sodium salts

(ii) Basic dyes of Rhodamine series eg. Rhodamine 6G which are utilized as halogen salts.

THEORY OF ACTION OF ADSORPTION INDICATORS:--

The action of adsorption indicators is based upon the properties of colloids.

When a chloride solution is titrated with a solution of silver nitrate, the precipitated silver chloride adsorbs chloride ions (a precipitate has tendency to adsorb its own ions). It may be termed the primary adsorbed layer and it is held by secondary adsorption oppositely charged ions present in solution [shown diagrammatically in Figure 6(a)]

As soon as the stoichiometric point is reached, silver ions are present in excess.

These will now be primarily adsorbed and nitrate ions will held by secondary adsorption [as shown in Figure 6(b)]

If fluorescein is also present in the solution, then negative fluorescein ion, which is much more strongly adsorbed than the nitrate ion, is immediately adsorbed and will reveal its presence on the precipitate, not by its own colour, which is that of the solution, but by the formation of a pink complex of silver and a modified fluorescein ion on the surface with the first trace of excess of silver ions.

An alternative view is that during the adsorption of the fluorescein ion a rearrangement of the structure of the ion occurs with formation of a coloured substance.

It is important to notice that the colour change takes place at the surface of the precipitate. If chloride is now added, the suspension will remain pink until chloride ions are present in excess, the adsorbed silver will be the converted into silver chloride which will then primarily adsorb chloride ions. The fluorescein ions secondarily adsorbed will pass back into solution to which they impart a greenish-yellow colour.

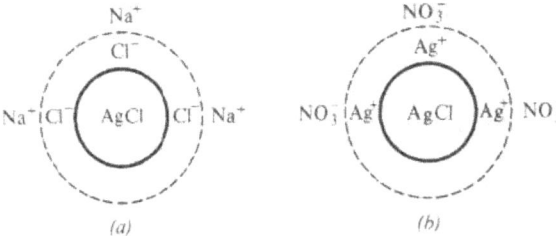

Fig-6:--(a) AgCl precipitated in the presence of excess of Cl⁻,

(b) AgCl precipitated in the presence of excess of Ag⁺

CONDITIONS REQUIRED FOR THE CHOICE OF A SUITABLE ADSORPTION INDICATOR:--

(1) The precipitate should separate as far as possible in the colloidal condition. The solution should not be too dilute otherwise less amount of precipitate will occur and sharp colour change may not be obtained at the end point.

(2) The indicator ion must be of opposite charge to the ion of the precipitating agent.

(3) The indicator ion should not be adsorbed before the particular compound has been completely precipitated but it should be strongly adsorbed immediately after the equivalence point.

(4) The indicator ion should not be too strongly adsorbed by the precipitate.

DISADVANTAGE OF ADSORPTION INDICATORS:--

Silver halides are sensitized to the action of light by a layer of adsorbed dyestuff. Due to this reason titrations should be carried out with a minium exposure to sunlight.

APPLICATION OF ADSORPTION INDICATORS

Or,

APPLICATION OF FAJAN'S METHOD OF ADSORPTION TITRATION:--

Or,

PROPERTIES AND USES OF ADSORPTION INDICATORS:--

Adsorption indicators are used for the estimation of followinghalide salts described in below Table by using standard solution of Silver nitrate as titrant in the presence of following acidic, basic or neutral solution:--

Sl. No.	Indicator	Use	Colour change of end point	Further data of interest or nature of solution
01	Fluorescein	Cl^-, Br^-, I^- with Ag^+	Yellowish green → pink	Solution must be neutral or weakly basic
02	Dichloro fluroescein	Cl^-, Br^-, BO_3^- with Ag^+	Yellowish green → red	Useful pH range 4.4 – 7.0
03	Eosin or tetrabromo fluorescein	Br^-, I^-, SCN^- with Ag^+	Pink → reddish violet	Best in acetic acid solution, useful down to pH 1-2
04	Rose Bengal or Dichlorotetraiodo fluorescein	I^- in presence of Cl^- with Ag^+	Red → Purple	Accurate if $(NH_4)_2CO_3$ added
05	Rhodamine 6G	Ag^+ with Br^-	Orange pink → reddish violet	Best in dilute (upto 0.3M) HNO_3

(4) TURBIDITY METHOD:--

Or,

GAY-LUSSAC-STAS METHOD:--

Turbidity method of precipitation titration or Gay-Lussac method is used for the determination of silver with chloride.

In this method a standard solution of sodium chloride is titrated with a solution of silver nitrate or vice versa. End point is confirmed without the use of indicator by finding no turbidity at the end of the titration when one of the standard solution of the substance is added to the standard solution of the other substance.

Further Gay-Lussac method had been modified by Gay-Lussac-Stas method. In this modification method standard solution of sodium chloride is added to the standard solution of silver nitrate in the presence of free nitric acid and a small quantity of pure barium nitrate.

METHOD:--

An accurate amount of 0.4g of silver nitrate is weighed into a well-stoppered 200cm^3 bottle.

Then 100ml. of water, few drops of concentrated nitric acid and a small crystal of barium nitrate are added and titrated with standard 0.1M sodium chloride by adding 20 ml. at once. Further bottleis stoppered and shaken vigorously until the precipitate of silver chloride gets coagulated. and a clear solution is obtained after settling of precipitate.

Taken volume of sodium chloride solution should leave the silver still in excess. Addition of chloride solution is continued, 1cm^3 at a time, stoppering and shaking after each addition until no tubidity is produced.

Total volume of sodium chloride solution is noted.

The determination is repeated by using a fresh sample of silver nitrate of about the same weight and run in initially that volume of the 0.1M sodium chloride, less than 1ml, which the first titration has indicated will be required and after that chloride solution is added dropwise.

End point is being determined within one drop.

Note:--

MODIFICATION OF VOLHARD'S METHOD OF PRECIPITATION TITRATION:--

(1) Modified Volhads method of precipitation titration is used for determination of chlorides, bromides and iodides in acid solution ie., nitric acid.

During the process of determination excess of standard solution of silver nitrate is added to the standard solution of sodium chloride. Further a definite amount of nitrobenzene is added as coagulant to prevent the interaction of silver chloride precipitate with silver thiocyanate as silver thiocyanate is less soluble salt then silver chloride otherwise it may interfere the titration process and correct sharp colour change may not be obtained at the end of the titration.

$$AgNO_3 + NaCl \longrightarrow AgCl + NaNO_3$$

or,

$$Ag^+ + Cl^- \rightleftharpoons AgCl$$

$$Ag^+ + SCN^- \rightleftharpoons AgSCN$$

Finally it is titrated with standard solution of 0.1M ammonium thiocyanate in the presence of ferric ammonium sulphate as indicator. At end point a reddish brown colour is obtained due to formation of ferrous thiocyanate.

$$AgCl + SCN^- \rightleftharpoons AgSCN + Cl^-$$

$$Fe^{3+} + SCN^- \longrightarrow (FeSCN)^{2+}$$

(2) Modified Volhard's method of precipitation titration is also used for determination of chlorinated compounds in benzoic acid, sodium benzoate and benzyl alcohol.

The silver chloride is precipitated in a warm solution in presence of amylacohol in order to cogulate the precipitate at the water-amyl alcohol interface and this prevents its interaction with ferric thiocyanate and avoids the need for filtration.

for example,

(1) DETERMINATION OF CHLORINATED COMPOUNDS IN BENZOIC ACID:--

METHOD:--

2g of benzoic acid is mixed with 50ml. of amyl alcohol in a dry flask and 3g of sodium is added.

The flask is connected to a reflux condenser. It is warmed gently until the evolution of hydrogen ceases.

It is boiled gently for one hour. The liquid is cooled to below 100° and 50ml. of water, 5 ml. of 0.1N silver nitrate and 20ml. of nitric acid are added. Then it is titrated with 0.1N ammonium thiocyanate by using solution of ferric ammonium sulphate as indicator. Not less than 4.2ml. of 0.1N ammonium thiocyanate is required.

(2) Modified Volhard method of precipitation titration also can be used for determination of chlorinated compounds in vinyl ether in similar manner as discussed under the determination of chlorinated compounds in benzoic acid.

(3) Modified Volhard method is also used in the assay of chlorbutol and dicophane where silver chloride is precipitated in a solution containing a small amount of nitrobenzene and the mixture is

well shaken before titration with standard solution of 0.1N ammonium thiocyanate by using ferric ammonium sulphate as indicator.

ESTIMATION OF SODIUM CHLORIDE:--

PRINCIPLE:--

Sodium chloride can be assayed with the help of Volhard's method of precipitation titration.

During the process of the assay, at first sodium chloride solution reacts with excess amount of 0.1N silver nitrate solution in presence of nitric acid and provides a white precipitate of silver chloride.

$$NaCl + AgNO_3 \rightarrow AgCl + NaNO_3$$

After that excess of silver nitrate is titrated with standard solution of 0.1N ammonium thiocyanate solution in presence of ferric ammonium sulphate, $NH_4Fe(SO_4)_2 12H_2O$ as indicator and provides a white precipitate of silver thiocyanate.

$$AgNO_3(excess) + NH_4SCN \rightarrow AgSCN \downarrow + NH_4NO_3$$

Silver chloride is more soluble than silver thiocyanate so it may react with silver thiocyanate and may provide a precipitate of silver thiocyanate.

$$Ag^+ + SCN^- \rightarrow AgSCN \downarrow$$

So it becomes necessary to remove silver chloride by filtration or treating with immiscible liquid like nitrobenzene or dibutyl phthalate as coating material which forms a layer over the precipitate of silver chloride.

At the end of the titration, ferric ion obtained from ferric ammonium sulphate combines with standard solution of ammonium thiocyanate and provides a reddish brown colour due to formation of ferrous thiocyanate.

$$Fe^{3+} + SCN^- \rightleftharpoons [FeSCN]^{2+}$$

NOTE:--

Nitric acid is added to prevent precipitation of silver carbonate, silver phosphate and hydrolysis of ferric salt.

METHOD:--

0.1 g of sodium chloride is weighed and dissolved in 50 ml. of water in a glass stoppered flask.

50.0 ml. of 0.1 M silver nitrate, 5 ml of 2M nitric acid and 2 ml. of dibutyl phthalate are added, shaken well and titrated with 0.1M ammonium thiocyanate using 2ml. of ferric ammonium sulphate solution as indicator, until the colour becomes reddish yellow.

Each ml. of 0.1M silver nitrate is equivalent to 0.005844 g of NaCl

PREPARATION AND STANDARDISATION OF STANDARD SOLUTION OF 0.1M AgNO₃ AND 0.1M NH₄SCN:--

(I)

(A) PREPARATION OF 0.1M SILVER NITRARE:--17.0 g of silver nitrate is dissolved in sufficient water to produce 1000 ml.

(B) STANDARDISATION OF 0.1M AgNO₃ SOLUTION:-- 0.1 g of sedum chloride is dried at 110°C for 2 hours and dissolved in 5 ml. of water. 5 ml. of acetic acid, 50 ml. of methnol and 0.15 ml. of eosin solution are added. It is stirredd preferably with magnetic stirrer and titrated with 0.1M silver nitrate solution.

Each ml. of 0.1M silver nitrate is equivalent to 0.005844 g of NaCl.

(II)

(A) PREPARATION OF 0.1 M AMMONIUM THIOCYANATE:-- 7.612 g of ammonium thiocyanate is dissolved in sufficient water to produce 1000 ml.

(B) STANDARDISATION OF 0.1M AMMONIUM THIOCYANATE:--30.0 ml. of 0.1M silver nitrate is taken into a glass stopperd flask and diluted with 50 ml. of water.

Then 2ml. of nitric acid and 2ml. of ferric ammonium sulphate solution are added and titrated with 0.1M ammonium thiocyanate solution to the first appearance of a red-brown colour.

Each ml. of 0.1M silver nitrate is equivalent to 0.007612 g of NH₄SCN.

(b)COMPLEXOMETRIC TITRATION:--

Complexometric titration is such type of titration which is used for the determination of metal salts like zinc sulphate,lead acetate by the use of different methods like Direct titration method in thepresence of 0.05M Disodium edetate as titrant, hexamine buffer and xylenol orange indicator,for the determinationof calcium chloride, calcium gluconate by the use of Replacement titration method in the presence of 0.05 disodium edetate titrant, ammonia –ammonium chloride buffer and mordant black II mixture indicator, for the determination of aluminium hydroxide gel,alum by the use of back titration methodin the presence of 0.05M Plumbous nitrate titrant,hexamine buffer and xylenol orange indicator by getting different colours at the end point of titration and finally amount or percentage purity of unknown metal salt is determined with the help of proper formula and I.P.factor.

At the end of complexometric titration a water soluble stable complex is formed by transforming a simple metal ion into complex ion by the addition of the reagent.

During the process of Complexometric titration, a substance donates the electrons to metal ions by which a coordinate linkage is formed, known as ligand.

Complexometric titration can be explained by taking an example of determination of magnesium sulphate by using replacement titration in the presence of standard solution of 0.05M disodium edetate as titrant, ammonia-ammonium chloride buffer and mordant black mixture as metal-ion indicator.

During the process of the assay, disodium edetate ionizes into sodium cation and edetate anion in the presence of aqueous solution and further edetate anion combines with magnesium cation obtained by the ionization of magnesium sulphate and finally a water soluble complex of magnesium sulphate is obtained with the appearance of blue colour as end point.

EDTA (ethylene diamine tetraacetic acid) can be assigned by formula H_4Y,

So,

disodium edetate can be written as Na_2H_2Y.

Na_2H_2Y ionizes into H_2Y^{2-} in aqueous solution.

$$NaH_2Y \rightleftharpoons 2Na^+ + H_2Y^{2-}$$

$H2Y^{2-}$ reacts with all metals in a 1:1 ratio.

The reaction with cations, M^{2+} can be written as such:--

$$M^{2+} + H_2Y^{2-} \rightleftharpoons MY^{2-} + 2H^+$$

or,

$$Mg^{++} + H_2Y^{2-} \rightleftharpoons MgY^{2-} + 2H^+$$

Or,

For other cations, the reactions can be expressed as such:--

$$M^{n+} + H_2Y^{2-} \rightleftharpoons (MY)^{n-4} + 2H^+$$

$$M^{3+} + H_2Y^{2-} \rightleftharpoons MY^- + 2H^+$$

$$M^{4+} + H_2Y^{2-} \rightleftharpoons MY + 2H^+$$

One mole of the complex forming H_2Y^{2-} reacts in all cases with one mole of the metal ion and in each case, two moles of hydrogen ion are formed.

It is clear from above equation that the dissociation of complex is governed by the pH of the solution.

If pH of the solution is lowered then stability of metal-EDTA complex is decreased. The more stable complex can be found at minimum pH for selected metals in following manner:--

STABILITY WITH RESPECT TO pH OF SOME METAL-EDTA COMPLEX:--

Minimum pH at which complexes exist	Selected metals
1-3	$Zn^{4+}, Bi^{3+}, Fe^{3+}$
4-6	$Pb^{2+}, Cu^{2+}, Zn^{2+}, Fe^{2+}, Al^{3+}, Ni^{2+}$
8-10	$Ca^{2+}, Ba^{2+}, Mg^{2+}, Sr^{2+}$

It has been seen that EDTA complexes with divalent metal ions are stable in alkaline or slightly acidic solutions which complexes with tri and tetra valent metal ions may exist in solutions of much higher acidity.

The reaction in between magnesium sulphate with standard solution of disodium edetate can be represented in following manner also:--

Disodium edetate ⇌ Edetate ion

$+Mg^{++} \rightarrow$ Mg-EDTA $+2H^+$

PREPARATION OF 0.05 M DISODIUM EDETATE:--

18.6g of disodium edetate is dissolved in sufficient water to produce 1000ml.

STANDARDIZATION OF 0.05M DISODIUM EDETATE:---

About 0.8g of granulated zinc is dissolved in 12ml. of dilute hydrochloric acid and 0.1ml. of bromine water by gentle warming. It is boiled to remove excess bromine, cooled and sufficient water is added to produce 200.0ml. Then 20ml. of resulting solution is taken in a flask and nearly neutralized with 2M sodium hydroxide. After that it is diluted to about 150ml. with water and sufficient ammonia buffer pH 10.0 is added to dissolve the precipitate and 5ml. is added in excess. 50mg of mordant black II mixture is added and titrated with the disodium edetate solution until the solution turns green.

Each ml. of 0.05M disodium edetate is equivalent to 0.000654g of Zn.

DIFFERENT TERMS USED IN COMPLEXOMETRIC TITRATION:--

(1) COORDINATION ENTITY:--

A coordination entity constitutes a central metal atom or ion bonded to a fixed number of ions or molecules.

For example,

$[COCl_3(NH_3)_3]$ is a co ordination entity in which the cobalt ion is surrounded by three ammonia molecules and three chloride ions.

(2) CENTRAL ATOM/ION:--

When a fixed number of ions/groups are bound in a definite geometrical arrangement around the atom/ion in a coordination entity then such atom/ion is called the central atom or ion.

For example;

$[NiCl_2(H_2O)_4], [COCl(NH_3)_5]^{2+}$ and $[Fe(CN)_6]^{3-}$

Coordination entities contain Ni^{2+}, CO^{3+} and Fe^{3+} central atom or ion.

(3) LIGANDS:--

The ions or molecules bound to the central atom or ion in the coordination entity are called ligands.

Ligand can be either a neutral molecule or a charged ion.

Ligand may be simple ions such as Cl^-, small molecules such as H_2O or NH_3, larger molecules such as $H_2NCH_2CH_2NH_2$ or $N(CH_2CH_2NH_2)_3$ or even macromolecules such as protein.

Ligand molecule usually possess oxygen, nitrogen or sulphur in their structure.

Ligand molecule contains atleast one lone pair of electrons by which a co-ordinate linkage takes place with metal ions.

CLASSIFICATION:--

On the basis of the number of points of attachment to the metal ion, ligand can be classified into following types:--

(I) UNIDENTATE OR MONODENTATE:--

when ligand is bound to the metal ion at only one point by the donation of a lone pair of electrons to the metal then such ligand is known as unidentate or monodentate.

Examples:--

Halide ion or Cl^-, molecules like H_2O or NH_3, CN^- are monodentate.

Hg^{++} and Cl$^-$ yield [HgCl$^+$], HgCl$_2$, [HgCl$_3$]$^-$ and [HgCl$_4$]$^-$

Ag$^+$ & CN$^-$ yield AgCN

(ii) BIDENTATE OR DIDENTATE:--

when the ligand molecule or ion has two atoms, each of which has a lone pair of electrons, then the molecule has two donor atoms and it may be possible to form two coordinate bonds with the same metal ion; such a ligand is said to be bidentate.

Example:--

(a) H$_2$NCH$_2$CH$_2$NH$_2$ (Ethane -1, 2-diamine) or ethylene diamine

ethylene diamine can coordinate through two nitrogen atoms.

(b) H$_2$N-CH$_2$-COOH, Glycine can coordinate through the oxygen of the COOH group and the nitrogen of the NH$_2$ group.

(iii) MULTIDENTATE OR POLYDENTATE:--

when several donor atoms are present in a single ligand or they contain more than two coordinating atoms permolecule then such ligands are known as polydentate.

Example:--

Ethylene diamine tetra acetic acid which has two donor nitrogen atoms and four donor oxygen atoms in the molecule.

$$\begin{array}{c} \text{HOOCH}_2\text{C} \\ \diagdown \\ \text{N}\!-\!\text{CH}_2\!-\!\text{CH}_2\!-\!\text{N} \\ \diagup \\ \text{HOOCH}_2\text{C} \end{array} \begin{array}{c} \text{CH}_2\text{COOH} \\ \diagup \\ \\ \diagdown \\ \text{CH}_2\text{COOH} \end{array}$$

Ethylene diamine tetra acetic acid is also known as hexadentate.

(4) CHELATE LIGAND:--

When a di or polydentate ligand uses its two or more donor atoms to bind a single metal ion, known as chelate ligand.

Example:-- Ethylene diamine tetra acetic acid.

(5) COMPLEXING AGENT:--

They are such agents which chelate with metals.

Example:-- Ethylene diamine tetra acetic acid or EDTA.

(6) CHELATES:--

They are such agents or compounds which result from combination of an electron donor (like N, O or S) with metal ion to form a ring structure.

Example:-- Calcium edetate.

$^-OOCH_2C-N(\ldots)N-CH_2COO^-$ ... Ca ... or ... (structure)

(7) SEQUESTERING AGENTS:--

They are such type of water soluble chelating agents which form water-soluble chelates with metal ion.

Example:--EDTA or edetic acid or sequestrene and disodium edetate.

(8) COMPLEXONE OR COMPLEXONE III:--

They are such type of agents which contain the group – $N(CH_2COOH)_2$ and they chelate with di, tri and tetra-valent cations to form complexes containing strainless 5-membered rings.

Example:--Disodium edetate;

$NaOOCH_2C\diagdown N-CH_2-CH_2-N\diagup CH_2COONa$
$HOOCH_2C\diagup \qquad \qquad \qquad \diagdown CH_2COOH$

METAL ION INDICATORS:--

Metal ion indicators are such type of indicators which are used in complexometric titrations when metal ions are titrated with a standard solution of disodium edetate as a titrant.

During the process of complexometric titration, metal-ion indicator combines with metal ions and forms metal-indicator complex and further metal-in complex is more stable than M-In complex.

At the equivalence point, free metal ions are not present and thus free indicator ion shows a colour which is different from the colour of M-In complex.

$\quad$ M $\quad$ + $\quad$ In $\longrightarrow$ M - In
Metalion $\quad$ Indicator $\quad$ Metal - Indicator complex

$\quad$ M $\quad$ + $\quad$ EDTA $\longrightarrow$ M - EDTA
Metal ion $\quad$ Complexing agent $\quad$ Metal - EDTA complex

Examples:--

(1) Mordant black II or Eriochrome Black I or Solochrome black, Chemically known as sodium 1-(1- hydroxy-2-naphthylazo)-6-nitro-2-naphthol-4-sulphonate (II)

ii) [Structure of Mordant black II showing naphthalene ring with NaO$_3$S group at position 4, OH at position 2 (labeled 1), azo linkage (N=N) at position 1 (labeled 2) connecting to a second naphthalene ring with OH group, and O$_2$N at position 6]

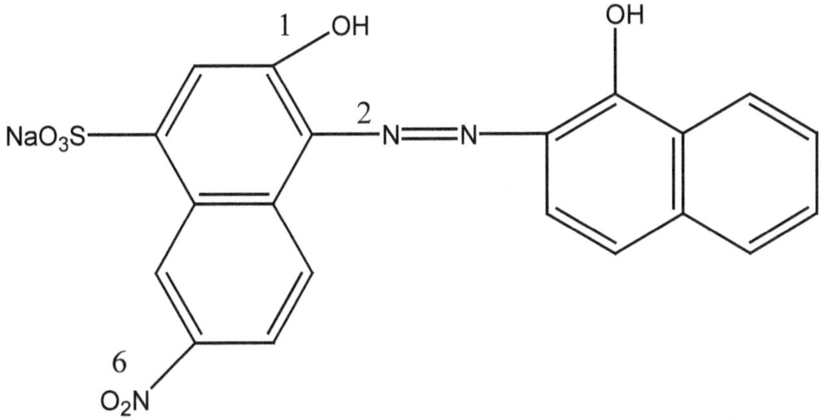

(2) Xylenol orange

(3) Murexide

(4) Catechol violet

(5) Bromopyrogallol red

TYPES OF COMPLEXOMETRIC TITRATION:--

Or,

DETECTION OF END POINT IN COMPLEXOMETRIC TITRATION:--

DIRECT TITRATION:--

(1) Direct titration is such type of complexometric titration where metal ion is directly titrated with standard solution of EDTA by using suitable buffer solution and metal ion indicator by buffering the metal ion solution to the desired pH (for example, pH-10 with ammonia-ammonium chloride buffer).

An auxiliary complexing agent like triethanolamine is used to prevent precipitation of the hydroxide of the metal.

Example:--

Direct titration is used for the determination of zinc sulphate, lead acetate, strong lead subacetate solution and lead monoxide by using xylenol orange indicator for metallic ions in acid solution and hexamine buffer at an acid pH and 0.05M disodium edetate as titrant. Xylenol orange indicator has lemon yellow colour in acid solution and produces red complexes with metals.

(2) BACK TITRATION:--

Back titration is such type of complexometric titration which can be used for such metals which cannot be titrated directly. They may precipitate from the solution in the pH range necessary for the titration or they may form inert complexes or they may form complexes too slowly or a suitable metal indicator is not available.

In such cases an excess of standard EDTA solution is added, the resulting solution is buffered to the desired pH and the excess of the reagent is back titrated with a standard metal ion solution like zinc chloride or zinc sulphate or magnesium chloride or magnesium sulphate or plumbous nitrate by using suitable metal indicator like xylenol orange or dithizone.

Examples:--

(1) Back titration is used for the determination of aluminium hydroxide gel, alum, dried aluminium hydroxide gel and aluminium hydroxide tablets by using hexamine buffer, xylene orange indicator and 0.05M solution of plumbous nitrate as titrant.

(2) As per USP Back titration is also used for the determination of aluminium by using a mixture of acetic acid and ammonium acetate as buffer, dithizone as indicator and 0.05M zinc sulphate solution as titrant.

(3) REPLACEMENT OR SUBSTITUTION TITRATION--

Replacement titration is such type of complexometric titration which is used for the determination of such metals ions which do not react or react unsatisfactorily with a metal indicator or they provide a poor end point when titrated directly.

Replacement titration is also used for such metal ions which form EDTA complex that are more stable then those of other metals such as magnesium and calcium.

The metal cation M^{n+} to be determined may be treated with the magnesium complex of EDTA when the following reaction occurs.

$$M^{n+} + MgY^{2-} \rightleftharpoons (MY)^{(n-4)+} + Mg^{2+}$$

The amount of magnesium ion set free is equivalent to the cation present and can be titrated with a standard solution of EDTA and a suitable metal indicator.

Examples:--

(1) Replacement titration is used for determination of calcium chloride, calcium lactate, calcium lactate tablets, calcium gluconate injection, calcium gluconate in the presence of ammonia and ammonium chloride buffer, mordant black II indicator and standard solution of magnesium sulphate. Buffer is used to maintain the pH at about 10 and indicator provides a blue colour at pH 7-11 and forms red complexes with metals.

During the process of the determination, four complexes are formed in the order of decreasing stability ie., calcium edetate, magnesium edetate, magnesium-indicator, calcium indicator.

During the titration edetate reacts first with the free calcium ions, then with the free magnesium ions and finally with the magnesium-indicator complex.

Thus at the endpoint the colour changes from wine-red to clear blue.

At the end of the titration, volume of 0.05 magnesium sulphate must be subtracted from the volume of 0.05M disodium edetate.

(4) ALKALIMETRIC TITRATION:--

When a solution of disodium ethylene diamine tetra acetate, Na_2H_2Y is added to a solution containing metallic ions, complexes are formed with the liberation of two equivalents of hydrogen ion:

$$M^{n+} + HY^{2-} \rightleftharpoons (MY)^{(n-4)+} + H^{2+}$$

The hydrogen ions can be titrated with a standard solution of sodium hydroxide using an acid base indicator or a potentiometric end point.

Alternatively, an iodate-iodide mixture is added as well as the EDTA solution and the liberated iodine is titrated with a standard solution of thiosulphate. Metal solution should be neutralized before titration.

(5) MISCELLANEOUS METHODS:--

(a) Halide ions like Cl^-, Br^-, I^{2-} and thioyanate ion SCN^- can be determined by precipitation as silver halide like silver bromide, silver iodide and silver thiocyanate. Further it is dissolved in tetracyano nickelate.

(b) Ion i.e., $[Ni(CN)_4]^{2-}$ and equivalent amount of nickel is determined by rapid titration with EDTA using an appropriate indicator i.e., murexide.

(c) Sulphate can be determined by precipitation as barium sulphate or as lead sulphate. The precipitate is dissolved in an excess of standard EDTA solution and the excess of EDTA is back – titrated with a standard magnesium or zinc solution using solochrome black as indicator.

(d) Phosphate can be determined by precipitating as $Mg(NH_4)PO_4,6H_2O$, dissolving the precipitate in dilute hydrochloric acid, adding an excess of standard EDTA solution, buffering at pH-10 and black titrating with standard magnesium ions solution in the presence of solochrome black.

MASKING AND DEMASKING AGENT:--

MASKING AGENT:--

Masking can be defined as the process in which a substance, without physical separation of it or its reaction products, is so transformed that it does not enter into a particular reaction.

Masking agent is used to determine metal ions like Ca^{2+}, Mg^{2+}, Pb^{2+} and Mn^{2+} in the presence of metals like Cd, Zn, Hg(II), Cu, Co, Ni, Ag and Pt by masking with an excess of potassium or sodium cyanide.

Example:--

Cyanide ion (potassium cyanide or sodium cyanide)

$$M^{2+} + 4CN^- \longrightarrow [M(CN)_4]^{2-}$$

Where M = Cd, Zn or Cu

Hence, it is possible to determine cations like Ca^{++}, Mg^{2+}, Pb^{++} and Mn^{2+} in presence of Cd, Zn, Cu, Co, Ni metals by masking with an excess of potassium or sodium cyanide.

DEMASKING AGENT:--

Demasking is the process in which the masked substance regains its ability to enter into a particular reaction.

Demaksing agent is used for the determination of Mg, Zn and Cu.

During the process of demasking, cyanide complexes of zinc and cadmium may be demasked with formaldehyde-acetic acid solution or better with chloral hydrate.

$$[Zn(CN)_4]^{2-} + 4H^+ + 4HCHO \longrightarrow Zn^{2+} + 4HOCH_2CN$$

Determination of Mg, Zn and Cu can be performed by titrating metal solution in following manner:--

(i) An excess of standard EDTA is added and back titrated with standard Mg solution using solochrome black (Eriochrome black T) as indicator. This provides the sum of all the metals like Mg, Zn, and Cu present.

(ii) Analiquot portion is treated with excess of KCN and titrated as before. This gives Mg only.

(iii) Excess of chloral hydrate is added to the titrated solution in order to liberate the Zn from the cyanide complex and titrated until the indicator turns blue. This gives the Zn only. The Cu content only then be found by differences.

ESTIMATION OF MAGNESIUM SULPHATE:--

PRINCIPLE:--

Magnesium sulphate can be assayed by means of direct titration of complexometric determination.

During the process of the assay, magnesium sulphate is titrated with standard solution of 0.05M disodium edetate in the presence of strong ammonia-ammonium chloride buffer and mordant black mixture indicator. Magnesium ion combines with edetate ion and forms a complex of magnesium edetate.

Disodium edetate   Edetate ion

Mg-EDTA

METHOD:--

0.3g of magnesium sulphate is dissolved in 50ml of water. 10ml of strong ammonia-ammonium chloride solution is added and titrated with 0.05M disodium edentate solution by using 0.1g of mordant black II mixture as indicator until a blue colour is obtained.

Each ml of 0.05M disodium edetate is equivalent to 0.00602g of $MgSO_4$

ESTIMATION OF CALCIUM GLUCONATE:--

PRINCIPLE:--

Calcium gluconate can be estimated with the help of complexometric replacement titration method.

When calcium gluconate is titrated alone with standard solution of 0.05M disodium EDTA then a poor end point is obtained. So, 0.05M Magnesium sulphate solution is used which favours replacement process and a sharp colour change is obtained at the end point in the presence of mordant black-II mixture indicator and strong ammonia solution.

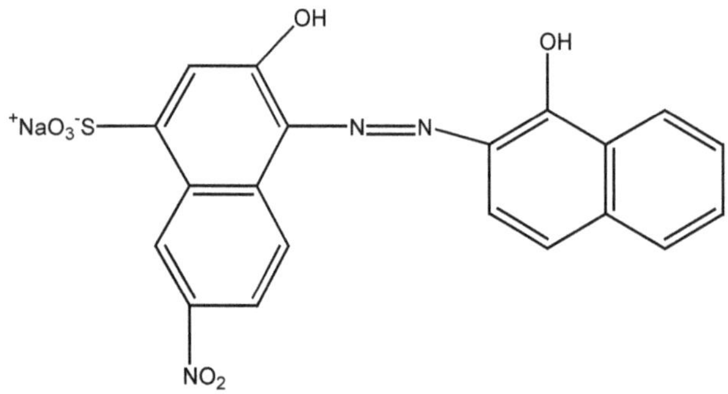

Mordant black-II mixture indicator

At first EDTA react with free calcium ions. Then it reacts with Magnesium ions.

$$Ca^{2+} + H_2Y^{2-} \rightleftharpoons CaY^{2-} + 2H^+$$
Edetate ion

$$Mg^{2+} + H_2Y^{2-} \rightleftharpoons MgY^{2-} + 2H^+$$

Finally it reacts with magnesium – indicator complex

$$Mg^2D^- \text{ (red)} + H_2Y^{2-} \rightleftharpoons MgY^{2-} + H^2D^- \text{ (blue)} + H^+$$

Where D^- = anion of mordant black-II mixture indicator

Since the magnesium-indicator complex is wine red in colour and the free indictor is blue between pH 7 and 11, the colour of the solution changes from wine-red to blue at the end-point.

Another titration is carried out with same quantity of reagent under same condition without calcium gluconate. The difference gives the amount of disodium edetate consumed by the calcium gluconate.

The above reaction also can be written in extended manner:--

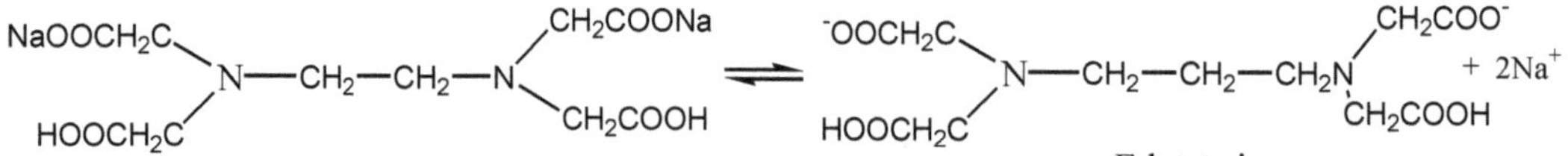

[Reaction scheme: Edetate ion + Ca²⁺ ⇌ Calcium edetate complex + 2H⁺]

[Reaction scheme: Edetate ion + Mg²⁺ ⇌ Magnesium edetate complex + 2H⁺]

METHOD:--

0.5g of calcium gluconate is taken in a conical flask and dissolved in 50 ml. of warm water. Then it is cooled. 5.0 ml. of 0.05M magnesium sulphate and 10ml of strong ammonia solution are added. Then it is titrated with 0.05 M disodium edetate using mordant black II mixture as indicator. Reading is noted as (A)

The experiment is repeated with same reagents except calcium gluconate and reading of disodium edetate solution is noted as (B).

The difference (A – B) gives the amount of disodium edetate required by the sample.

Each ml. of the 0.05 M disodium edetate is equivalent to 0.02242 g of $C_{12}H_{22}CaO_{14}$, H_2O.

$$\text{Percentage purity of calcium gluconate} = \frac{\text{Volume of disodium EDTA required (A-B)} \times \text{Molarity of EDTA} \times 0.02242 \times 100}{\text{Weight of calcium gluconate} \times 0.05}$$

GRAVIMETRY:-

PRINCIPLE:--

Gravimetry analysis or quantitative analysis by weight is the process of isolating and weighing of an element or a definite compound in as a pure form as possible. The element or compound is separated from a weighed portion of the substance. A large proportion of the determinations in gravimetric analysis is concerned with the transformation of the element or radical into a pure stable compound which can be readily converted into a form suitable for weighing. The weight of the element or radical may be readily calculated from a knowledge of the formula of the compound and the atomic weights of the constituent elements.

The separation of the element or of the compound can be done by different following methods:--

(1) Precipitation methods

(2) Volatilization methods

(3) Electroanalytical methods

(4) Extraction and chromatographic methods

(1) PRECIPITATION METHODS OR TECHNIQUES:--

Precipitation method is mainly used for gravimetric analysis.

During precipitation methods of gravimetric analysis, the constituent is precipitated from solution in a form which is so slightly soluble that no appreciable loss occurs when the precipitate is separated by filtration and weighed.

EXAMPLES:--

(a) DETERMINATION OF SILVER:--

A solution of the substance is treated with an excess of Sodium or Potassium chloride solution. The precipitate is filtered off, well washed to remove soluble salts, dried at 130-150°C and weighed as Silver chloride. Frequently the constituent is weighed in a form other than that in which it was precipitated.

(b) DETERMINATION OF MAGNESIUM:--

A solution of the substance is treated with Dilute ammonia solution and Ammonium chloride solution in the presence of Disodium hydrogen phosphate and it provides a precipitate of Magnesium ammonium phosphate; $Mg(NH_4)PO_4, 6H_2O$. Further it is weighed and ignited. Finally Magnesium is determined from ignited product of Magnesium pyrophosphate, $Mg_2P_2O_7$ by the knowledge of formula of compound and the atomic weights of the constituent elements.

FACTORS AFFECTING PRECIPITATION METHOD OF GRAVIMETRIC ANALYSIS:--

(1) The precipitate must be so insoluble that no appreciable loss occurs when it is collected by filtration. It should not exceed 0.1mg.

(2) The physical nature of the precipitate must be such that it can be readily separated from the solution by filtration and can be washed free of soluble impurities.

(3) The precipitate must be convertible into a pure substance of definite chemical composition. This may be affected either by ignition or by a simple chemical operation such as evaporation with a suitable liquid.

THE PURITY OF THE PRECIPITATE:--

(A) CO-PRECIPITATION:--

When a precipitate separates from a solutionthen it is not always perfectly pure. It may contain varying amounts of impurities dependent upon the nature of the precipitate and the conditions of precipitation. The contamination of the precipitate by substances which are normally soluble in mother liquor is termed co-precipitation.

TYPES OF CO-PRECIPITATION:--

(1)First type of co-precipitation

(2)Second type of co-precipitation

(1) FIRST TYPE OF CO-PRECIPITATION:--

First type of co-precipitation is concerned with adsorption at the surface of the particles exposed to the solution. This type is greatest for gelatinous precipitates and least for macro-crystalline character. Precipitates with ionic lattices confirm Paneth-Fajans-Hahn adsorption rule which states that the ion that is most strongly adsorbed by an ionic substance (crystal lattice) is that ion which forms the least soluble salt. Thus on sparingly soluble sulphates calcium ions are adsorbed preferentially over magnesium ions because calcium sulphate is less soluble than magnesium sulphate.

Also silver iodide adsorbs silver acetate much more strongly than silver nitrate under comparable conditions since silver iodide is the less soluble.

The deformability of the adsorbed ions and the electrolyte dissociation of the adsorbed compound also have influence; the smaller the dissociation of the compound,the greater is theadsorption. So, hydrogen sulphide being weak electrolyte is strongly adsorbed by metallic sulphides.

(2) SECOND TYPE OF CO-PRECIPITATION:--

Second type of co-precipitation relates to the occlusion of foreign substances during the process of crystal growth from the primary particles.

The second type of co-precipitation may be visualized as occurring during the building up of the precipitate from the primary particles due to a certain amount of surface adsorption and during their coalescence the impurities will either be partially eliminated if large single crystals are formed and the process takes place slowly or if coalescence is rapid, large crystals compound of loosely bound small crystals may be produced and some of the impurities may be entrained within the walls of the large crystals. If the impurity is isomorphous or forms a solid solution with the precipitate, the amount of co-precipitation may be very large.

Example:--

Precipitation of Barium sulphate in the presence of alkali nitrates due to formation of solid solutions.

(B) POST-PRECIPITATION:--

Post precipitation is such type of precipitation which occurs on the surface of the first precipitate after its formation. It occurs with sparingly soluble substances which form super saturated solutions. They usually have an ion in common with the primary precipitate.

Examples:--

(i) During the precipitation of calcium as oxalate in the presence of magnesium, magnesium oxalate separates out gradually upon the calcium oxalate, the longer the precipitate is allowed to stand in contact with the solution.

(ii) During the precipitation of copper or mercury (II) sulphide in 0.03M hydrochloric acid in the presence of zinc ions; zinc sulphide is slowly post-precipitated.

DIFFERENCE BETWEEN CO-PRECIPITATION AND POST PRECIPITATION:--

SL.No.	Co-precipitation	Post-precipitation
01.	The contamination decreases with the time that the precipitate is left in contact with the mother liquor	The contamination increases with the time that the precipitate is left in contact with the mother liquor
02.	Contamination decreases the faster the solution is agitated by either mechanical or thermal means	Contamination increases the faster the solution agitated by either mechanical or thermal means
03.	The magnitude of contaminations is less	The magnitude of contamination is more.

VARIOUS STEPS INVOLVED IN GRAVIMETRIC ANALYSIS:--

The following steps are involved in gravimetric analysis as in case of determination of chloride as silver chloride:--

(1) WEIGHING OF PRIMARY SUBSTANCE:--

0.2g of sodium chloride is weighed accuratcly into a 250ml. beaker provided with a stirring rod and covered with a clock glass.

(2) MIXING OFSUBSTANCE WITH SOLVENT AND OTHER MEDIUM SOLUTION:--

About 150ml. of water is added, stirred until the solid is dissolved. Then 0.5ml. of concentrated nitric acid is added.

(3) ADDITION OF OTHER REACTANT:--

Then sufficient amount of 0.1M silver nitrate is added to the cold solution slowly till no further precipitate is obtained. The determination is carried out in subdued light.

(4) HEATING OF SUSPENSION:--

Suspension is heated nearly to boiling with constant stiring till the precipitate coagulates and the supernatant liquid becomes clear.

(5) DRYING OF FILTERING CRUCIBLE:--

Filtering crucible is dried at 130-150°C.

(6) COOLING OF CRUCIBLE:--

Crucible is allowed to cool in a desicator.

(7) COLLECTION OF PRECIPITATE:--

The precipitate is collected in the weighed filtering crucible.

(8) WASHING OF PRECIPITATE:--

The precipitate is washed two or three times by decantation with about 10ml. of cold very dilute nitric acid before transferring the precipitate to crucible.

(9) REMOVAL OF SILVER CHLORIDE:--

Last small particles of silver chloride are removed adhering to the beaker with a policeman.

(10) WASHING OF PRECIPITATE:--

The precipitate is washed in the crucible with very dilute nitric acid added in small portions until 3-5ml. of the washings collected in a test tube, give no turbidity with 1 or 2 drops of 0.1M hydrochloric acid.

(11) PLACING OF CRUCIBLE AND CONTENTS IN OVEN:--

Crucible and contents are placed in an oven at 130-150°C for 1 hour.

(12) COOLING AND WEIGHING OF CRUCIBLE:--

Further crucible is allowed to cool in a desccator and weighed.

Then heating a cooling is repeated until constant weight is obtained.

(13) CALCULATION OF PERCENTAGE OF CHLORINE:--

Percentage of chlorine is calculated present in the sample by the use of following calculation:-

The calculation of weight of a constituent in a given precipitate follows directly from the proportion.

Mn Ap : n M :: w : x

Where Mn Ap = molecular weight of precipitate

M = Atomic (or molecular) weight of the element (or radical) n = Number of atomic or molecular weights of M in the molecular weight Mn Ap

w = Weight of precipitate and

x = weight of constituent desired further if w is the weight of the sample used,

The percentage of the constituent sought y can be given by

x : w : : y : 100

or,

$$y = \frac{x \times 100}{w}$$

Example:--

1.0g of chloride compound, after suitable treatment, yielded 0.15g of silver chloride, calculate the percentage of chlorine in the compound.

Solution:--

AgCl : Cl : : 0.15 : x

(107.87 + 35.45) : 35.45 : : 0.15 : x

$$x = \frac{0.15 \times 35.45}{143.32} = 0.1236g$$

Now 0.1236 : 1 : : y : 100

Or, y = 0.1236 x 100

Or, y = 12.36 % of chloride.

PHARMACEUTICAL APPLICATION OF GRAVIMETRIC ANALYSIS:--

1) Gravimetric analysis is used to calibrate other instruments to get accurate and highly corrected data in reference to standards.

2) It is used to determine the plasma volume by using Radio iodinated human serum albumin and red blood cells.

3) It is used to determine chloride in a given mixture.

4) Solvent extraction-gravity method is used to determine fat content

5) It is used to diagnose organic matter by a gravimetric method such as to determine cholesterol in nicotine, wheat, corn and barley with salicylate pesticides to make lactose, drug of milk products.

6) It is used to deterine Magnesium ions levels in water.

7) It is used to assess inorganic ash content of polymer.

8) It is used to determine inorganic anions and cations.

9) It is used to determine sulphur dioxide, carbon dioxide and iodine.

10) It is also used for determination of dicolfenac in pharmaceutical preparations.

ESTIMATION OF BARIUM SULPHATE:--

PRINCIPLE:--

Barium sulphate can be estimated by the use of precipitation method of gravimetric analysis.

During the process of estimation, barium sulphate reacts with ammonium acetate and acetic acid in presence of potassium dichromate and urea and gets precipitated as barium dichromate which is collected as residue after drying at 105 degree Celsius.

$BaSO_4 + K_2Cr_2O_7 = BaCr_2O_7 + K_2SO_4$

METHOD:--

About 0.6g of Barium sulphate is weighed accurately in a platinum crucible. 5g of sodium carbonate and 5g of potassium carbonate are added and mixed. It is heated to 1000°c and maintained at this temperature for 15 minutes. It is allowed to cool and the residue is suspended in 150ml. of water.

The crucible is washed with 2ml. of acetic acid. Further it is added to the suspension.

It is cooled in ice and filtered by decantation by transferring as little of the solid matter as possible to the filter. The residue is washed with successive quantities of a 2% w/v solution of sodium carbonate until the washings are free from sulphate and the washings is discarded.

5ml. of dilute hydrochloric is added to the filter and washed through into the vessel containing the bulk of the solid matter with water. 5ml. of HCl is added and diluted to 100ml. with water. 10ml. of a 49% w/v solution of ammonium acetate, 25ml. of a 10% w/v solution of potassium dichromate and 10g of urea are added.

It is covered and digested in an oven at 80° to 85° for 16 hours and filtered while still hot through a sintered-glass filter (porosity no.4) The precipitate is washed initially with a 0.5% w/v solution of potassium dichromate and finally with 2ml. of water. It is dried to constant weight at 105°.

Each gram of residue is equivalent to 0.9213g of $BaSO_4$

UNIT-IV

REDOX TITRATIONS:--

(a) CONCEPTS OF OXIDATION AND REDUCTION OR REDOX REACTION:--

Oxidation and redox reactions can be explained with the help of following three concepts:--

(1) Classical idea of redox reactions

(2) Redox reactions in terms of electron transfer reactions.

(3) Oxidation number.

(1) CLASSICAL IDEA OF REDOX REACTIONS:--

(a) OXIDATION:--

oxidation can be defined as the addition of oxygen/electronegative element to a substance or removal of hydrogen/ electropositive element from a substance.

Example:--

(i) ADDITION OF OXYGEN:--

$2Mg + O_2 \longrightarrow 2MgO$

$CH_4 + 2O_2 \longrightarrow CO_2 + 2H_2O$

Here magnesium is oxidized into magnesium oxide and methane is oxidized into carbon dioxide where oxygen element has been added.

(ii) REMOVAL OF HYDROGEN:--

$2H_2S + O_2 \longrightarrow 2S + 2H_2O$

Here hydrogen sulphide oxidizes into sulphur by the process of removal of hydrogen.

(iii) ADDITION OF ELECTRO NEGATIVE ELEMENT:--

$Mg + Cl_2 \longrightarrow MgCl_2$

Here magnesium oxidises into magnesium chloride by the addition of chlorine element.

(iv) REMOVAL OF ELECTRO POSITIVE ELEMENT:--

$2K_4[Fe(CN)_6] + H_2O_2 \longrightarrow 2K_3[Fe(CN)_6] + 2KOH$

Here potassium electro positive element is removed from potassium ferrocyanide and changes into potassium ferricyanide.

(B) REDUCTION:--

Reduction can be defined as removal of oxygen/electronegative element from a substance or addition of hydrogen/electropositive element.

i) $2HgO \xrightarrow{\Delta} 2Hg + O_2$

(Removal of oxygen from mercuric oxide)

ii) $2FeCl_3 + H_2 \longrightarrow 2FeCl_2 + 2HCl$

(removal of electronegative element, chlorine from ferric chloride)

iii) $CH_2 = CH_2 + H_2 \longrightarrow H_3C - CH_3$

(addition of hydrogen)

iv) $2HgCl_2 + SnCl_2 \longrightarrow Hg_2Cl_2 + SnCl_4$

(addition of electropositive element, mercury to mercuric chloride).

In this reaction, stannous chloride also oxidizes into stannic chloride by addition of electronegative element, chlorine on it. It indicates that oxidation and reduction occur simultaneously.

(2) REDOX REACTION IN TERMS OF ELECTRON TRANSFER REACTIONS:--

OXIDATION:--

Oxidation reaction involves loss of electrons by any species.

REDUCTION:--

Reduction reaction involves gain of electrons by any species.

OXIDIZING AGENT OR OXIDANT:--

Oxidizing agent accepts electrons from species and it reduces.

REDUCING AGENT OR REDUCTANT:--

Reducing agent donates electros to the elements and it oxidizes.

Examples :

1) Sodium chloride ionizes in aqueous solution in following manner.

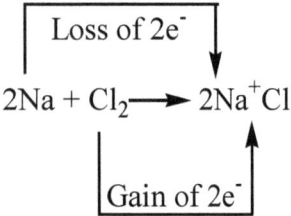

Above reaction can be written as half reaction :

$2Na \longrightarrow 2Na^+ + 2e^-$

$Cl_2 + 2e^- \longrightarrow 2Cl^-$

Sum of half reactions,

$2Na + Cl_2 \longrightarrow 2Na^+Cl^-$ or $2NaCl$

Here sodium metal oxidizes into sodium cation by the loss of two electrons and chlorine atom reduces into chloride anion by the gain of two number of electrons.

(3) OXIDATION NUMBER:--

Oxidation number of an element is a number which applied to that element in a particular compound, indicates the amount of oxidation or reduction which is required to convert one atom of the element from the free state to that in the compound. If oxidation is necessary, to effect the change, then oxidation number is positive and if reduction is necessary, then oxidation number is negative.

The following rules are applied to the determination of oxidation numbers:--

(1) The oxidation number of the free or uncombined element is zero.

(2) The oxidation number of hydrogen (except in certain hydriates) has a value of +1.

(3) The oxidation number of oxygen (except in peroxides) is -2.

(4) The oxidation number of a metal in combination (except in hydrides) is usually positive.

(5) The oxidation number of a radical or ions is that of its electrovalency with the correct sign attached, i.e., is equal to its electrical charge.

The oxidation number of a compound is always zero and is determined by the sum of the oxidation number of the individual atoms each multiplied by the number of atoms of the element in the molecule.

By the application of above rules, oxidation number of the desired element in a molecule or in ion can be determined.

It is clear that the metallic elements have positive oxidation number and non-metallic elements have positive or negative oxidation number.

The atoms of transition elements usually display several positive oxidation states.

oxidation number denotes the oxidation state of an element in a compound.

Examples:--

In CO_2, the oxidation state of carbon is +4 and that is also its oxidation number. Oxidation state as well as oxidation number of oxygen is -2.

The oxidation number/state of a metal in a compound is sometimes presented by stock notation. According to this, the oxidation number is expressed by putting a Roman numeral respresenting the oxidation number in parenthesis after the symbol of the metal in the molecular formula.

Examples:--

Aurous chloride and auric chloride are written as Au(I) Cl and Au(III)Cl$_3$. Similarly, stannous chloride and stannic chloride are written as Sn(II)Cl$_2$ and Sn (IV) Cl$_4$.

This change in oxidation number implies change in oxidation state which in turn helps to identify whether the species is present in oxidized form or reduced form.

Thus, Hg(I)Cl$_2$ is the reduced form of Hg(II) Cl$_2$ and it is the reduced form of Hg(II) Cl$_2$

The idea of oxidation number is applied to define oxidation, reduction, oxidizing agent (oxidant), reducing agent (reductant) and the redox reaction.

(a) OXIDATION:-- An increase in the oxidation number of the element in the given substance.

(b) REDUCTION:--A decrease in the oxidation number of the element in the given substance.

(c) OXIDISING AGENT:--A reagent which can increase the oxidation number of an element in a given substance. These reagents are also called as oxidants.

(d) REDUCING AGENTS:--A reagent which lowers the oxidation number of an element in a given substance. These reagents are also called as reductants.

Redox reactions:--Reactions which involve change in oxidation number of the interacting species.

Example:--

i) $2\overset{0}{H_2} + \overset{0}{O_2} \longrightarrow 2\overset{+1\ -2}{H_2O}$

Oxidation number of hydrogen increases from 0 to +1 and oxidation number of oxygen reduces from 0 to -2. So, hydrogen oxidizes to water molecule where oxygen reduces to water molecule.

ii) $\overset{0}{H_2} + \overset{0}{Cl_2} \longrightarrow 2\overset{+1\ -1}{HCl}$

Here, hydrogen oxidizes whereas chlorine reduces.

iii) $\overset{-4}{C}\overset{+1}{H_4} + 4\overset{0}{Cl_2} \longrightarrow \overset{+4}{C}\overset{-1}{Cl_4} + 4\overset{+1}{H}\overset{-1}{Cl}$

Methane oxidizes into carbon tetrachloride as oxidation number of carbon increases from –4 to +4.

Chlorine reduces into hydrochloric acid as oxidation number of chlorine decreases from 0 to – 1

(b) TYPES OF REDOX REACTION:--

(i) Combination reactions

(ii) Decomposition reactions

(iii) Displacement reactions – further it can be subclassified into

(a) Metal displacement

(b) Non metal displacement

(iv) Disproportionation reactions

(i) COMBINATION REACTIONS:--

Combination reaction is a combination of elements which form a redox reaction. Generally oxygen and other than oxygen also combine with other elements to form redox reaction.

Example:--

$\overset{0}{C} + \overset{0}{O_2} \overset{\Delta}{\longrightarrow} \overset{+4}{C}\overset{-2}{O_2}$

$3\overset{0}{Mg} + \overset{0}{N_2} \overset{\Delta}{\longrightarrow} \overset{+2}{Mg_3}\overset{-3}{N_2}$

(ii) DECOMPOSITION REACTION:--

Decomposition reaction is such type of reaction where a compound breaksdown into two or more components at least one of which must be in the elemental state.

Examples :

$2\overset{+1}{H_2}\overset{-2}{O} \overset{\Delta}{\longrightarrow} 2\overset{0}{H_2} + \overset{0}{O_2}$

$2\overset{+1}{Na}\overset{-1}{H} \overset{\Delta}{\longrightarrow} 2\overset{0}{Na} + \overset{0}{H_2}$

(iii) DISPLACEMENT REACTIONS:--

Displacement reaction is such type of reaction where an ion (or an atom) in a compound is replaced by an ion (or an atom) of another element.

(a) METAL DISPLACEMENT:--

A metal in a compound can be displaced by another metal in the uncombined state.

Examples :

$$\overset{+2\ +4\ -2}{CuSO_4} + \overset{0}{Zn} \longrightarrow \overset{0}{Cu} + \overset{+2\ +4\ -2}{ZnSO_4}$$

Here CuSO4 acts as reducing agent and oxidizes into copper whereas zinc metal acts as oxidizing agent and reduces into zinc sulphate.

$$\overset{+3\ -2}{Cr_2O_3} + 2\overset{0}{Al} \longrightarrow \overset{+3\ -2}{Al_2O_3} + 2\overset{0}{Cr}$$

Chromium oxide reduces into chromium whereas aluminium oxidizes into aluminium oxide.

(b) NON-METAL DISPLACEMENT:--

The non- metal displacement redox reaction include hydrogen displacement.

All alkali metals and some alkaline earth metals like Ca being good reductants displace hydrogen from cold water.

$$2\overset{0}{Na} + 2\overset{+1\ -2}{H_2O} \longrightarrow 2\overset{+1\ -2\ +1}{NaOH} + \overset{0}{H_2}$$

$$\overset{0}{Ca} + 2\overset{+1\ -2}{H_2O} \longrightarrow \overset{+2\ -2\ +1}{Ca(OH)_2} + \overset{0}{H_2}$$

(iv) DISPROPORTIONATION REACTIONS:--

It is such type of redox reaction where an element in one oxidation state is simultaneously oxidized and reduced.

Example:--

i) $2\overset{+1\ -2}{H_2O_2} \longrightarrow 2\overset{+1\ -2}{H_2O} + \overset{0}{O_2}$

Here oxygen of peroxide which is present in -1 state and is converted into zero oxidation state in O_2 and decreases to -2 oxidation state in H_2O.

So, hydrogen peroxide oxidizes to oxygen and reduces to water molecule.

(ii) Phosphorous undergoes disproportionation in the alkaline medium.

$$\overset{0}{P_4} + 3OH^- + 3H_2O \longrightarrow \overset{-3}{PH_3} + 3\overset{+1}{H_2PO_2^-}$$

Here phosphorous oxidizes into hypophospjorous acid and reduces into phosphine gas.

THEORY OF REDOX TITRATIONS:--

    Or,

PRINCIPLE OF OXIDATION-REDUCTION TITRATIONS:--

Or,

CHANGE OF ELECTRODE POTENTIAL DURING THE TITRATION OF A REDUCTANT WITH AN OXIDANT:--

Theory of redox titration can be explained by taking an example of titration of 100cm³ of 0.1N ferrous sulphate or iron(II) with 0.1N cerric ammonium sulphate or cerium (IV) in presence of dilute sulphuric acid.

$$\overset{4+}{Ce} + \overset{2+}{Fe} \rightleftharpoons \overset{3+}{Ce} + \overset{3+}{Fe}$$

Concentration of ferrous salt can be calculated with the help of change of electrode potential by titrating with standard solution of cerium (IV) in presence of dilute sulphuric acid. A reversible redox reaction can be written in following form as such.

Oxidant + ne $\rightleftharpoons$ Reductant

    or,

ox + ne $\rightleftharpoons$ Red

When an inert electrode is immersed in a solution containing both oxidant and reductant then electrode potential can be given by following expression.

$$E_T = E^\theta + \frac{RT}{nF} \ln \frac{a_{ox}}{a_{Red}}$$

where E_T= observed potential of the redox electrode at temperature T relative to the standard hydrogen electrode taken as zero potential.

E^θ= standard reduction potential

n = number of electrons gained by the oxidant is being concerted into the reductant a_{ox} and a_{red} are the activities of the oxidant and redutant respectively.

R = Gas constant

T = Absolute temperature

F = Faraday constant.

Since activities are difficult to determine directly, so they can be replaced by concentrations. Then equation becomes.

$$E_T = E^\theta + \frac{RT}{nF} \ln \frac{(ox)}{(Red)}$$

This equation is also known as Nernst equation. Substituting known values of R and F and changing from natural to common logarithms we have for a temperature of 25°C (T = 298K)

$$E25° = E^\theta + \frac{0.0591}{n} \log \frac{[ox]}{[Red]}$$

If the concentrations of the oxidant and reductant are equal, $E25° = E^\theta$, i.e., the standard reduction potential.

The quantity corresponding to [H$^+$] in acid base titrations is the ratio $\frac{[ox]}{[Red]}$

We are here concerned with two systems, the $\frac{Fe^{3+}}{Fe^{2+}}$ ion electrode (1) and the $\frac{Ce^{4+}}{Ce^{3+}}$ ion electrode (2)

For (1) at 25°C,

$$E_1 = E_1^\theta + \frac{0.0591}{1} \log \frac{[Fe^{3+}]}{[Fe^{2+}]}$$

$$= +0.75 + 0.0591 \log \frac{[Fe^{3+}]}{[Fe^{2+}]}$$

For (2) at 25°C,

$$E_2 = E_2^\theta + \frac{0.0591}{1} \log \frac{[Ce^{4+}]}{[Ce^{3+}]}$$

$$= 1.45 + 0.0591 \log \frac{[Ce^{4+}]}{[Ce^{3+}]}$$

The equilibrium constant of the reaction is given by

$$\log k = \log \frac{[Ce^{3+}] \times [Fe^{3+}]}{[Ce^{4+}] \times [Fe^{2+}]} = \frac{1}{0.0591} (1.45 - 0.750)$$

= 11.84

Or, k = 7 x 10^{11}

Since,

a ox$_1$ + b Red$_{II}$ ⇌ b ox$_{II}$ + a Red$_1$

Or, $\log \frac{[ox_{II}]^b \times [Red_1]^n}{[Red_{II}]^b \times [ox_1]^a} = \log k = \frac{n}{0.0591} (E_1^\theta - E_2^\theta)$

During the addition of the cerium (IV) solution upto the equivalence point, its only effect will be to oxidize the iron (II) (since k is large) and consequently change the ratio $\left[\frac{Fe^{3+}}{Fe^{2+}}\right]$

When 10cm³ of the oxidizing agent have been added,

$\frac{[Fe^{3+}]}{[Fe^{2+}]} = \frac{10}{90}$ (approx)

and $E_1 = 0.75 + 0.0591 \log \frac{10}{90}$

$= 0.75 - 0.056$

$= 0.69$ volt

With 50 cm³ of the oxidizing agent, $E_1 = E_2^\theta = 0.75$ volt,

With 90cm³, $E_1 = 0.75 + 0.0591 \log \frac{90}{10} = 0.81$ volt,

With 99cm³, $E_1 = 0.75 + 0.0591 \log \frac{99}{1} = 0.87$ volt,

With 99.9cm³, $E_1 = 0.75 + 0.0591 \log \frac{99.9}{1} = 0.93$ volt

At the equivalence point (100cm³)

$[Fe^{3+}] = [Ce^{3+}]$ and $[Ce^{4+}] = [Fe^{2+}]$ and the electrode potential is given by

$$\frac{E_1^\theta + E_2^\theta}{2} = \frac{0.75 - 1.45}{2} = 1.10 \text{ volts}$$

Since,

$a\ ox_I + b\ Red_{II} \rightleftharpoons b\ ox_{II} + a\ Red_I$

the potential at the equivalence point is given by

$$E_0 = \frac{bE_1^\theta + aE_2^\theta}{a + b}$$

Where E_1^θ refers to ox_1, Red_1 and E_2^θ to ox_{II}, Red_{II}

The subsequent addition of cerium (IV) solution will merely increase the ratio $[Ce^{4+}]/[Ce^{3+}]$

Thus,

With 101.0cm³, $E_1 = 1.45 + 0.0591 \log \frac{0.1}{100} = 1.25$ volts

With 101cm³, $E_1 = 1.45 + 0.0591 \log \frac{1}{100} = 1.33$ volts

With 110cm³, $E_1 = 1.45 + 0.0591 \log \frac{10}{100} = 1.39$ volts

With 190cm³, $E_1 = 1.45 + 0.0591 \log \frac{90}{100} = 1.45$ volts

These results are shown in following figure:--

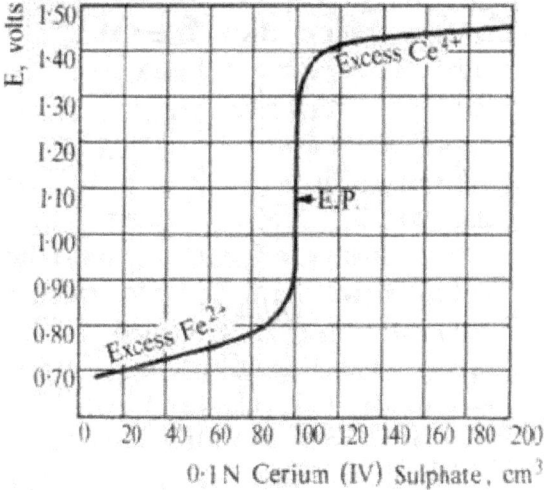

Fig.7:-- Titration of 100cm³ of 0.1M-iron (II) with 0.1M cerium culphate.

It is of interest to calculate the iron(II) concentration in the neighbourhood of the equivalence point.

When 99.9cm³ of the cerium(IV) solution have been added,

$$[Fe^{2+}] = 0.1 \times \frac{0.1}{199.9} = 5 \times 10^{-5} \text{ or } pFe^{2+} = 4.3$$

The concentration at the equivalence point is given by

$$\frac{[Fe^{3+}]}{[Fe^{2+}]} = \sqrt{k} = \sqrt{7 \times 10^{11}} = 8.4 \times 10^5$$

Since,

a ox$_I$ + b Red$_{II}$ ⇌ b ox$_{II}$ + a Red$_I$

$$\frac{[Red_1]}{[ox_1]} = \frac{[ox_{II}]}{[Red_{II}]} = \sqrt[a+b]{k}$$

Now,

$[Fe^{3+}] = 0.05N$

Hence,

$$[Fe^{2+}] = \frac{5 \times 10^{-2}}{8.5 \times 10^5} = 6 \times 10^{-8} N$$

Or,

pFe^{2+} = 7.2

Upto the addition of 101.0 cm^3 of cerium (IV) solution, the reduction potential is 1.27 volts. The [Fe^{3+}] is practically unchanged at 5 x 10^{-2} N and we may calculate [Fe^{2+}] with sufficiency accuracy for our purpose from the equations

$$E_1 = E_1^\theta + 0.0591 \, log \frac{[Fe^{3+}]}{[Fe^{2+}]}$$

$$1.27 = 0.75 + 0.0591 \, log \frac{[5 \times 10^{-2}]}{[Fe^{2+}]}$$

[Fe^{2+}] = 1 x 10^{-10}

Or, pFe^{2+} = 10

Thus, pFe^{2+} changes from 4.3 to 10 between 0.1 % before and 0.1% after the stoichiometric end – point.

It is clear that the abrupt change of the potential in the neighborhood of the equivalence point is dependent upon the standard potentials of the two oxidation reduction systems that are involved and therefore upon the equilibrium constant of the concentrations unless these are extremely small.

DETECTION OF END POINT IN OXIDATION REDUCTION TITRATION

Or,

REDOX TITRATIONS

Or,

TYPES OF REDOX TITRATIONS

Or,

DIFFERENT REDOX INDICATORS USED IN REDOX INDICATORS USED IN REDOX TITRATIONS:--

Or,

PRINCIPLES AND APPLICATIONSOF REDOX TITRATIONS:--

There are four types of redox titration:--

(1) Internal oxidation-reduction indicators used redox titration

(2) Self redox indicators used redox titrations or the reagent may serve as its own indicator type redox titration.

(3) External redox indicators used redox titrations

(4) Potentiometric methods redox type redox titration.

There are three types of redox indicator:--

(1) Internal redox indicators

(2) Self redox indicators or the reagent may serve as its own indicator

(3) External redox indicators

(1) INTERNAL OXIDATION-REDUCTION INDICATORS:--

An oxidation-reduction indicator should mark the sudden change in the oxidation potential in the neighbourhood of the equivalence point in an oxidation-reduction titration.

An ideal oxidation-reduction indicator has an oxidation potential intermediate between that of the solution titrated and that of the titrant and which exhibits a sharp, readily detectable colour change.

A redox indicator is a compound which exhibits different colours in the oxidized form and reduced forms.

$$\text{In}_{ox} + ne \rightleftharpoons \text{In Red}$$

The oxidation and reduction should be reversible. At a potential E the ratio of the concentrations of the two forms is given by the Nernst equation.

$$E = Eln^\theta + \frac{RT}{nF} \ln \frac{a_{Inox}}{a_{Inred}}$$

$$E \approx Eln^\theta + \frac{RT}{nF} \ln \frac{[I_{nox}]}{[In_{Red}]}$$

Where Eln^θ = the standard potential of the indicator.

(i) If the colour intensities of the two forms are comparable a practical estimate of the colour - change interval corresponds to the change in the ratio $\frac{In\ ox}{In\ Red}$ from 10 to 1/10; this leads to an interval of potential of

$$E = Eln^\theta \pm \frac{0.0591}{n} \text{ volts at } 25°C$$

(ii) If the colour intensities of the two forms differ considerably then intermediate colour is attained at a potential some what removed from Eln^θ, but the error is unlikely to exceed 0.06 volt.

(iii) For a sharp colour change at the end point, Eln^θ should differ by about at least 0.15 volt from the standard potentials of the other systems involve in the reaction.

Examples:--

1, 10 – phenanthroline iron(II) complex

Or,

1, 10 – phenanthroline iron (II) sulphate

Or,

Ferroin : $[Fe(C_{12}H_8N_2)_3]^{2+}$

Or,

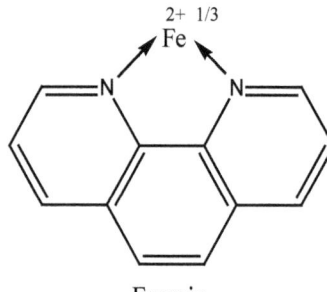

Ferroin

Ferroin indicator is prepared by dissolving 0.7g of ferrous sulphate and 1.5g of 1,10 phenanthroline hydrochloride in 70ml. of water and by adding sufficient water to produce 100ml.

1,10 phenanthroline iron(II) complex or ferroin indicator is used for the determination of ferrous sulphate solution which is titrated with standard solution of ceric ammonium nitrate by forming a pale blue colour at the end of the titration in presence of dilute sulphuric acid, colour changes from deep red to pale blue at a redox potential of 1.12 volts.

$$Ce^{4+} + Fe^{2+} \rightleftharpoons Ce^{3+} + Fe^{3+}$$

$$[Fe(C_{12}H_8N_2)_3]^{3+} + e^- \rightleftharpoons [Fe(C_{12}H_8N_2)_3]^{2+}$$
    Pale blue   Deep red
    (oxidised form)   (reduced form)

(2)

5-Nitro-1, 10-Phenanthroline iron (II)-sulphate

Or,

nitroferroin

5-nitro-1, 10-phenanthroline iron (II) sulphate

Nitroferroin is used as suitable internal redox indicator for the assay of ceric ammonium nitrate solution in the presence of ferrous sulphate solution at formal potential of 1.25 volts. in the presence of nitric acid or perchloric acid.

At the end point a pale blue colour (oxidized form) is obtained from red colour (reduced form).

(3) 4,7-dimethyl ferroin or 4,7-dimethyl-1,10-phenanthroline iron(II):--

4,7-dimethyl ferroin indicator is used for the determination of potassium dichromate with ferrous sulphate solution in the presence of 0.05M sulphuric acid at formal potential of 0.88 volts. At end point a pale blue colour (oxidized form) is obtained from red colour (reduced form)

(4) Diphenyl amine:--

Diphenyl amine internal redox indicator (0.1%) is used for the titration of iron (II) with potassium dichromate solution in the presence of concentrated sulphuric acid. An intense blue - violet colouration is produced at the end point at formal potential of 0.76 volts.

Diphenyl amine (I) at first oxidizes into colourless diphenylbenzidine (II) which is real indicator and reversibly oxidizes into diphenylbenzidine violet(III).

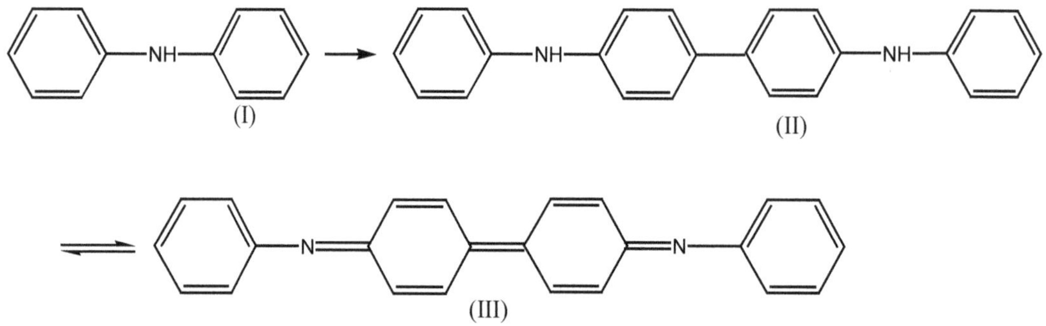

[Structures (I), (II), (III) of diphenylbenzidine oxidation]

(5) Diphenylbenzidine is also used for the titration of iron (II) with potassium dichromate solution in the presence of concentrated sulphuric acid. An intense blue-violet colouration is produced at the end point at formal potential of 0.76 volts.

(6) Methylene blue can be used as internal redox indicator for the titration of titanous chloride in the presence of acidic medium. At the end point blue colour (oxidized form) is obtained from colourless (reduced form) at formal potential of 0.52 volts.

(2) THE REAGENT MAY SERVE AS ITS OWN INDICATOR

Or,

SELF REDOX INDICATOR:--

(1) Potassium permanaganate is used as reagent or oxidizing agent or self redox indicator for the titration of hydrogen peroxide solution in the presence of dilute sulphuric acid medium. Potassium permanganate reduces into manganese sulphate by the gain of 05 no of electrons whereas hydrogen peroxide oxidizes into oxygen molecule by the loss of two number of electrons.

$$MnO_4^- + 8H^+ + 5e^- \rightleftharpoons Mn^{2+} + 4H_2O \quad \text{-------------- (I)}$$

$$H_2O_2 \rightleftharpoons 2H^+ + O_2 + 2e^- \quad \text{----------- (II)}$$

By multiplying equation I and Equation II by 2 and 5, we get

$$2MnO_4^- + 16H^+ + 10e^- \rightleftharpoons 2Mn^{2+} + 8H_2O$$

$$5H_2O_2 \rightleftharpoons 10H^+ + 5O_2 + 10e^-$$

Net equation,

$$2MnO_4^- + 6H^+ + 5H_2O_2 \rightleftharpoons 2Mn^{2+} + 8H_2O + 5O_2$$

(2) Cerium (IV) sulphate solution is used as self redox indicator for the determination of ferrous salt solution in the presence of acidic medium. At the end point a red colour is obtained but colour change is not so marked as for potassium permanganate.

$$Ce^{4+} + Fe^{2+} \rightleftharpoons Ce^{3+} + Fe^{3+}$$

(3) Iodine solution also can be used as self redox indicator or reagent for the titration of sodium thiosulphate. At the end point a pale blue colour is obtained.

$$I_2 + 2Na_2S_2O_3 \rightleftharpoons 2NaI + Na_2S_4O_6$$

But colour change is not so marked as for potassium permanganate.

Self redox indicator titration method has the drawback that an excess of oxidizing agent is always present at the end point. So a blank determination should be made by performing standardization and determination under similar experimental conditions to get highest accuracy.

(3) EXTERNAL REDOX INDICATORS:--

(1) POTASSIUM HEXA CYANO FERRATE (III) SOLUTION:--

$K_3[Fe(CN)_6]$ is used as external redox indicator for the titration of iron (II) with standard potassium dichromate solution by the use of spot-test method.

Near the equivalence point, drops of the solution of iron(II) and potassium dichromate are removed and brought into contact with dilute freshly prepared potassium hexa cyanoferrate (III) solution on a spot plate. The end-point is reached when the drop first fails to give a blue colouration.

$$Cr_2O_7^{2-} + 14H^+ + 6e^- \rightleftharpoons 2Cr^{3+} + 7H_2O$$
$$Fe^{2+} \rightleftharpoons Fe^{3+} + e^-$$

Net equation,

$$Cr_2O_7^{2-} + 14H^+ + 6Fe^{2+} \rightleftharpoons 2Cr^{3+} + 6Fe^{3+} + 7H_2O$$

(2) Uranyl acetate $U_2(CH_3COO)_2, 2H_2O$ is used as external redox indicator for the titration of zinc ions with standard potassium hexacyanferrate (II) solution, $K_4[Fe(CN)6]$. At the end point a brown colour is obtained.

$$[Fe(CN)_6]^{4+} + 2Zn^{2+} = Zn_2[Fe(CN)_6]$$

At the end point brown colour is obtained due to formation of zinc hexacyanoferrate(II)

(4) POTENTIOMETRIC METHODS:--

Potentiometric method is used for such substances which are coloured or very dilute solutions where the indicator method is inapplicable or of limited accuracy.

Potentiometric method depends upon measurement of the e.m.f between a reference electrode and an indicator (redox) electrode at suitable intervals during the titration.

Example:--

Determination of iron (II) solution by titration with a standard potassium dichromate solution.

METHOD:--

A 250ml. of 0.1N potassium dichromate solution and a 250ml. of 0.1M ammonium iron (II) sulphate solution are prepared.25ml. of ammonium iron(II) sulphate solution is placed in a beaker. Further 25ml. of 2.5M sulphuric acid and 50ml. of water are added.The burette is charged with 0.1N potassium dichromate solution and a capillary extension tube is added.

A bright platinum electrode as indicator electrode and a standard calomel electrode as reference electrode are used. The stirrer is set in motion. Then titration is started. After each addition of the potassium dichromate solution the e.m.f of the cell is measured.

The end point is determined (i) from the potential volume curve and (ii) by the differential method.

The molarity of the ammonium iron (II) sulphate solution is calculated and this is compared with the value computed from the actual weight of solid employed in preparing the solution.

(1)

CERIMETRY:--

Cerimetry is such type of redox titration where cerium (IV) sulphate is used as a powerful **oxidizing agentfor the determination of various reducing substances** like copper, molybdate, tellurite, cerium(III) **in the presence of** only in**acidic medium.** It is stable over prolonged periods.

Cerium (IV) sulphate is also used for analysis of hydrogen peroxide, persulphate, nitrites, uranium, iron, oxalates etc.

PREPARATION OF 0.1 N CERIUM (IV) SULPHATE:-- 0.1N cerium (IV) sulphate can be prepared by dissolving 64 to 66g of ceric ammonium sulphate, $(NH_4)_4[Ce(SO4)_4]$, $2H_2O$ in amixture of 28ml. of concentrated sulphuric acid and 500ml. of water. Then volume is made upto 1 litre with distilled water.

STANDARDIZATION OF 0.1N CERIUM (IV) SULPHATE:--

0.1N cerium (IV) sulphate solution can be standardized with the help of arsenic (III) oxide. Cerium (IV) sulphate reacts with arsenic trioxide in the presence of sulphuric acid, sodium hydroxide, osmium tetraoxide and reduces into cerrous sulphate by the gain of one number of electron.

$$AS_2O_3 + H_2O \rightleftharpoons 2H_3ASO_3$$

$$2Ce^{4+} + H_3ASO_3 + H_2O \rightleftharpoons 2Ce^{3+} + H_3ASO_4 + 2H^+$$

METHOD:--

About 0.2g of arsenic (III) oxide is dried at 105°-110°C for 1-2 hours and transferred to a conical flask. Then 20ml. of about 2M sodium hydroxide solution is added and the mixture is warmed gently until the arsenic (III) oxide has completely dissolved. It is cooled to room temperature and 100ml. of water and 25ml. of 2.5M sulphuric acid are added.

Then 3 drops of 0.01M Osmium-tetroxide solution (0.25g osmium tetroxide in 100ml. of 0.05M sulphuric acid) and 0.5ml. of N-phenyl anthranilic acid indicator are added.

Finally it is titrated with the 0.1N cerium (IV) sulphate solution until the first sharp colour change occurs from orange red to very pale blue or yellowish green to purple respectively.

APPLICATION OF CERIUM (IV) SULPHATE:--

(1) DETERMINATION OF NITRITE:--

Cerium (IV) sulphate is used for determination of nitrites like sodium nitrite by titrating with standard solution of ceric ammonium sulphate in the presence of sulphuric acid and ferroin indicator.

Ceric sulphate acts as oxidizing agent and reduces into cerous sulphate by gain of one number of electron whereas sodium nitrite acts as reducing agent and oxidizes into sodium nitrate.

$$2Ce^{4+} + NO_2^- + H_2O \longrightarrow 2Ce^{3+} + NO_3^- + 2H^-$$

METHOD:--

1.5g of sodium nitrate is dissolved in 500ml. of boiled water in a graduated flask. Then 50ml. of 0.1N cerium (IV) sulphate is treated with 10ml. of dilute sulphuric acid in another conical falsk. Further 25ml. of sodium nitrite solution is added to this flask by a pipette. After 5 minutes excess of cerium (IV) sulphate is titrated with standard solution of 0.1N ceric ammonium sulphate by using ferroin indicator. Finally end point is determined.

(2) DETERMINATION OF HYDROGEN PEROXIDE:--

Cerium (IV) sulphate solution is also used for determination of hydrogen peroxide in presence of dilute sulphuric acid by using feroin as indicator.

$$2Ce^{4+} + H_2O_2 \rightleftharpoons 2Ce^{3+} + O_2 + 2H^+$$

Cerium (IV) sulphate acts as oxidizing agent and reduces into cerium (III) sulphate whereas hydrogen peroxide acts as reducing agent and oxidizes into oxygen

(2) IODIMETRY:--

PRINCIPLE:--

The direct iodometric titration method or iodimetry refers to titrations with a standard solution of iodine.

Iodimetry titration is generally used for the assay of sodium thiosulphate in the presence of starch solution as indicator.

Here Iodine acts as oxidizing agent and reduces into sodium iodide by the gain of two number of electrons whereas sodium thiosulphate acts as reducing agent and oxidizes into sodium tetrathionale by the loss of two number of electrons.

$$I_2 \rightleftharpoons 2I^- + 2e^-$$

$$2S_2O_3^{2-} + 2e^- \rightleftharpoons S_4O_6^{2-}$$

Net equation,

$$I_2 + 2S_2O_3^{2-} \longrightarrow 2I^- + S_4O_6^{2-}$$

Or,

$$I_2 + 2Na_2S_2O_3 \xrightleftharpoons[]{starch} 2NaI + Na_2S_4O_6$$

Starch is added towards the end of the titration and it reacts with iodine in presence of iodide to form an intensely blue-coloured complex which is visible at very low concentrations of iodine.

METHOD:--

0.5g of sodium thiosulphate is dissolved in 20ml. of water and titrated with 0.05M iodine (14g of iodine is dissolved in a solution of 36g of potassium iodide in 100ml. of water). Then 3 drops of hydrochloric acid is added and volume is made upto 1 liter with water by using starch solution added towards the end of the titration as indicator.

Each ml. of 0.05M iodine is equivalent to 0.02482g of $Na_2S_2O_3, 5H_2O$.

(3) IODOMETRY:--

PRINCIPLE:--

The indirect iodometric titration or iodometry deals with the titration of iodine liberated in chemical reactions.

(i) Iodometry titration is used for the standardization of sodium thiosulphate with potassium dichromate solution in the presence of hydrochloric acid. The liberated iodine is titrated with standard solution of sodium thiosulphate by using starch solution as indicator.

$$K_2Cr_2O_7 + 6KI + 14HCl \longrightarrow 3I_2 + 2CrCl_3 + 8KCl + 7H_2O$$

$$2Na_2S_2O_3 + I_2 \longrightarrow Na_2S_4O_6 + 2NaI$$

Here potassium dichromate acts as oxidizing agent and reduces into chromous chloride where as sodium thiosulphate acts as reducing agent and oxidizes into sodium tetrathionate. Iodine also acts as oxidizing agent and reduces into sodium iodide.

METHOD:--

0.125g of potassium dichromate is dissolved in 25ml. of water in a stoppered conical flask. Then 10ml. of hydrochloric acid and 2g of potassium iodide are added and 100ml. of water is added after 15 minutes. Further it is titrated with 0.1N sodium thiosulphate solution by using starch solution as indicator. At end point a bottle green colour is obtained.

$$Normality\ of\ sodium\ thiosulphate = \frac{Weight\ of\ potassium\ dichromate}{Consumed\ volume\ of\ sodium\ thiosulphate \times 0.04904}$$

2) Iodometry or indirect iodometric titration is also used for the determination of copper sulphate.

PRINCIPLE:--

Copper sulphate can be assayed with standard solution of sodium thiosulphate in the presence of potassium iodide and acetic acid by using starch solution as indicator.

Copper sulphate reacts with potassium iodide and liberates iodine in the presence of acetic acid. Then liberated iodine reacts with sodium thiosulphate and produces sodium iodide and sodium trtrathionate. Iodine acts as oxidizing agent and reduces into sodium iodide by the gain of two number of electrons. Sodium thiosulphate acts as reducing agent and oxidizes into sodium tetrathionate by the loss of two number of electrons.

$$2CuSO_4 + 4KI \longrightarrow 2CuI + 2K_2SO_4 + I_2$$

$$I_2 + 2Na_2S_2O_3 \longrightarrow Na_2S_4O_6 + 2NaI$$

or

$$I_2 + 2e^- \rightleftharpoons 2I^-$$

$$2S_2O_3^{2-} \rightleftharpoons S_4O_6^{2-} + 2e^-$$

Net equation,

$$I_2 + 2S_2O_3^{2-} \rightleftharpoons 2I^- + S_4O_6^{2-}$$

Potassium thiocyanate is also used to allow liberated iodine to undergo complete titration.

METHOD:--

1.0g of copper sulphate is dissolved in 50ml of water in a 250ml. glass stoppered flask. Then 5ml. of acetic acid and 3g of potassium iodide are added. Further the liberated iodine is titrated with standard solution of 0.1N sodium thiosulphate by the use of starch solution as indicator. A faint blue colour is obtained. Then 2 g of potassium thiocyanate is added and stirred well. Further titration is continued until blue colour disappears.

Each ml. of 0.1N $Na_2S_2O_3$ is equivalent to 0.02497g of $CuSO_4.5H_2O$.

(4) BROMOMETRY:--

Bromometry is such type of redox titration where standard solution of Potassium bromate is used as oxidizing agent for the determination of reducing agent by liberating free bromine in the presence of hydrochloric acid.

Potassium bromate is a powerful oxidizing agent which reduces smoothly to bromide salt in presence of acid and finally converted into free bromine by liberating yellow colour at the end point of titration in the presence of Naphthalene black 12B, xylidine ponceau and fuchsine

$$BrO_3^- + 5Br^- + 6H^+ \longrightarrow 3Br_2 + 3H_2O$$

PREPARATION OF 0.1N POTASSIUM BROMATE:--

2.784g of potassium bromate is dissolved in sufficient water to produce 1 litre.

APPLICATION OF BROMOMETRY:--

Bromometry is used for the determination of following compounds:--

(1) DETERMINATION OF ANTIMONY OR ARSENIC:--

The tirivalent arsenic or antimony can be determined by titrating with standard solution of 0.1N potassium bromate in the presence of hydrochloric acid andNaphthalene black 12B or xylidine ponceau as indicator.At the end point colourless or very pale yellow colour is obtained.

During the process of determination, potassium bromate being oxidizing agent reduces into hydrogen bromide and arsenic or antimony trioxide being reducing agent oxidizes into arsenic or antimony pentaoxide.

$$2KBrO_3 + 3AS_2O_3 + 2HCl \longrightarrow 2KCl + 2AS_2O_5 + 2HBr$$
$$\text{or} \qquad\qquad\qquad\qquad \text{or}$$
$$Sb_2O_3 \qquad\qquad\qquad\qquad Sb_2O_5$$

(2) DETERMINATION OF HYDROXYLAMINE:--

Hydroxylamine can be determined by titrating with standard solution of 0.1N potassium bromate in the presence of 5M-hydrochloric acid. Further excess of Potassium bromate is determined by titrating with standard solution of 0.1N sodium thiosulphate in the presence of definite amount of potassium iodide and starch solution as an indicator. Potassium bromate reduces into bromide salt and hydroxylamine oxidizes into nitrate salt. Further it provides free bromine which interacts with potassium iodide and provides iodine. Finally liberated iodine reacts with standard solution of sodium thiosulphate and provides sodium iodide and sodium tetrathionate at the end of the reaction.

$$NH_2OH + BrO_3^- \longrightarrow NO_3^- + Br^- + H^+ + H_2O$$

$$BrO_3^- + 5Br^- + 6H^+ \longrightarrow 3Br_2 + 3H_2O$$

$$Br_2 + 2KI \longrightarrow I_2 + 2KBr$$

$$I_2 + 2Na_2S_2O_3 \longrightarrow 2NaI + Na_2S_4O_6$$

(5) DICHROMETRY:-- Potassium dichromate is used as excellent primary standard substance. It is used as oxidizing agent generally for the determination of iron in iron ore whereas iron(III) content of ore oxidises into iron(II) in presence of hydrochloric acid and Potassium dichromate reduces into green Chromoium chloride salt. Further solution is titrated with standard dichromate solution.

$$Cr_2O_7^{2-} + 6Fe^{2+} + 14H^+ \rightleftharpoons 2Cr^{3+} + 6Fe^{3+} + 7H_2O$$

PREPARATION OF 0.0167M $K_2Cr_2O_7$ SOLUTION:--

4.9g of potassium dichromate is weighed which is previously powdered and dried in a desiccator for 4 hours. Then it is dissolved in sufficient water to produce 1000ml.

STANDARDISATION OF 0.016M $K_2Cr_2O_7$:--

Potassium dichromate can be standardized with the help of 0.1M sodium thiosulphate in the presence of acidic medium like 2M hydrochloric acid by using starch solution as indicator. During the process of standardization potassium dichromate reduces into bottle green colour of chromium chloride where as sodium thiosulphate oxidizes into sodium tetrathionate. At end point colour changes from dark blue to bottle green.

$$K_2Cr_2O_7 + 6KI + 14HCl = 3I_2 + 2CrCl_3 + 8KCl + 7H_2O$$

$$2Na_2S_2O_3 + I_2 = Na_2S_4O_6 + 2NaI$$

METHOD:--

1g of potassium iodide and 7ml. of 2M hydrochloric acid are added to 20ml. of 0.0167 M $K_2Cr_2O_7$ solution. Then 250ml. of water is added and titrated with 0.1M sodium thiosulphate in the presence of 3ml. of starch solution as indicator which is added towards the end of titration until the colour changes from blue to light green.

Each ml. of 0.1M sodium thiosulphate is equivalent to 0.0049g of $K_2Cr_2O_7$.

APPLICATION:--

DETERMINATION OF IRON(II):--

Iron (II) salt can be determined by titrating with 0.1N potassium dichromate solution in the presence of dilute H_2SO_4 acid and N- phenyl anthranilic acid (II) as internal indicator.

During the process of determination, potassium dichromate reduces into chromium sulphate whereas iron(II) solution oxidizes into Iron(III) salt. At end point colour changes from green to violet.

$Cr_2O_7^{2-} + 6Fe^{2+} + 14 H^+ \rightleftharpoons 2Cr^{3+} + 6Fe^{3+} + 7H_2O$

(6) TITRATION INVOLVING POTASSIUM IODATE:--

Potassium iodate is a powerful oxidizing agent and used for the determination of arsenic or antimony.

It is also used for determination of mercury, hydrazines, vandates etc.

PREPARATION OF 0.05M POTASSIUM IODATE:--

10.7g of potassium iodate, previously dried at 100°C to constant weight, is dissolved in sufficient water to produce 1000ml.

STANDARDIATION OF 0.05M POTASSIUM IODATE:--

Potassium iodate can be standardized with the help of standard solution of 0.1M sodium thiosulphate in the presence of 1M sulphuric acid by using starch solution as indicator.

Potassium iodate being oxidizing agent reduces into iodine whereas sodium thiosulphate acts as reducing agent and oxidizes into sodium tetrathionate.

Potassium iodate reduces into iodine in several stages --

$IO_3^- + 6H^+ + 6e^- \rightleftharpoons I^- + 3H_2O$

$IO_3^- + 5I^- + 6H^+ \longrightarrow 3I_2 + 3H_2O$

$I_2 + 2Na_2S_2O_3 \rightleftharpoons 2NaI + Na_2S_4O_6$

METHOD:--

25ml. of 0.05M potassium iodate solution is diluted to 100ml. with water and 20ml. of this solution is treated with 2g of potassium iodide followed by 10ml. of 1M sulphuric acid. Then liberated iodine is titrated with 0.1M sodium thiosulphate by using 1ml. of starch solution as indicator.

Each ml. of 0.1M sodium thiosulphate is equivalent to 0.03566g of KIO_3

APPLICATION:--

(1) DETERMINATION OF ARSENIC OR ANTIMONY:--

PRINCIPLE:--

The determination of arsenic in arsenic (III) compounds is based upon the following reaction:--

$$IO_3^- + 2H_3AsO_3 + 2H^+ + Cl^- = ICl + 2H_3AsO_4 + H_2O$$

Here Potassium iodate reduces into iodine monochloride where arsenic (III) compound oxides into arsenious acid and it gets oxidized into arsenic acid in the presence of sodium hydroxide and hydrochloric acid.

A similar reaction can be obtained with antimony (III) compounds.

METHOD:--

1.1g of arsenic trioxide is dissolved in 10% sodium hydroxide solution and volume is made upto 250ml. in a graduated flask. 25ml. water, 60ml. concentrated hydrochloric acid and 5ml. of chloroform are added to above 25ml. of solution. Then it is titrated with 0.1N potassium iodate till colour changes to pale brown. Further titration is continued till colour changes to faintly violet. Finally end point is obtained as colourless.

(2) DETERMINATION OF MERCURY:--

PRINCIPLE:--

Potassium iodate is also used for determination of mercury.

$$IO_3^- + 2Hg_2Cl_2 + 6H^+ + 13Cl^- \longrightarrow ICl + 4[HgCl_4]^{2-} + 3H_2O$$

Here potassium iodate reduces into iodine monochloride whereas mercury(II) chloride oxidizes into mercury(I) chloride in the presence of hydrochloric acid.

METHOD:--

2.5g of finely powdered mercury (II) chloride is dissolved in 100ml. water. 25ml. water, 2ml. N – hydrochloric acid and excess of 50 % phosphorous acid are added to 25ml. of above solution and allowed to stand for 12 hours or more.

Precipitate of mercury (I) chloride is filtered and washed with cold water.

30ml. concentrated hydrochloric acid, 20ml. water and 5ml. carbon tetrachloride are added to the precipitate and the mixture is titrated with standard 0.1N potassium iodate in usual manner as discussed under the determination of arsenic.

$$2HgCl_2 + H_3PO_3 + H_2O \longrightarrow Hg_2Cl_2 + 2HCl + H_3PO_4$$

UNIT-V

ELECTROCHEMICAL METHODS OF ANALYSIS:--

(a) CONDUCTOMETRY:--

INTRODUCTION:--

Conductometry is such type of analysis by which electrical conductivity of the solution is measured.

Electrical conductivity is obtained due to flow of electricity through solutions of electrolytes under the influence of migration of ions when potential difference is applied between the electrodes. The cations which are positively charged move towards the negatively charged electrode, known as CATHODE while the anions which are negatively charged move towards the positively charged electrode, known as ANODE.

The movement of anions and cations occurs in such a way that the solution remains electrically neutral through out the movement under the influence of electrical field. The mobility of ion is affected by factors like charge, size, mass and extent of solvation.

It is essential to know following terms to understand conductometry:--

(1) OHM'S LAW:--

It states that the strength of current flowing through a conductor is directly proportional to the potential difference applied across the conductor and inversely proportional to the resistance of the conductor

Hence, Ohm's law can be represented as such:--

$$I = \frac{E}{R}$$

Where I=current,

E=Potential difference

and R=Resistance

The current is measured in amperes, potential difference in volts and electrical resistant in ohms.

(2) CONDUCTANCE:--

Conductance implies the ease with which the current flows through a conductor. The conductance is the reciprocal of resistance.

$$C = \frac{1}{R}$$

Where,

C=conductance

The conductance is expressed in units of reciprocal of Ohms or Mhos.

(3) SPECIFIC RESISTANCE:--

Specific resistance can be defined as the resistance of a uniform column of the material of the conductor having a length of 1 cm and area of cross section of 1 sq cm.

$$e = R\frac{a}{l} = ohm\ \frac{(cm)^2}{cm} = ohm.cm$$

Specific resistance is expressed in ohm.cm

The Specific resistance also can be derived as such:--

The Resistance of the conductor is directly proportional to its length and inversely proportional to its area of cross section.

Thus,

$R \alpha\ l$ and $R \alpha\ \frac{1}{a}$,

where l=length,

a=area of cross section

Or, $R \alpha\ l/a$

Or, $R = \varrho\frac{l}{a}$

where ϱ is a constant called the specific resistance or resistivity.

If l = 1 cm and a = 1 sq cm

then

$$\varrho = R\ ohms$$

(4) SPECIFIC CONDUCTANCE:--

Specific conductance can be defined as "the specific conductance of any conductor is the reciprocal of specific resistance" and is denoted by k (small kappa)

As we know that

$$R = \varrho\frac{l}{a}$$

Or, $R = \frac{1}{k}.\frac{l}{a}$

Or, $k = \frac{1}{R}.\frac{l}{a}$ ohm^{-1}cm^{-1}

If L = 1 cm and a = 1 sq cm

then above equation can be written as

$$k = \frac{1}{R} = \varrho$$

Hence,

Specific conductance also can be defined as" the conductivity offered by a solution of length 1 cm and area of 1 sq cm cross section"

Specific conductance is expressed in mhos/cm

(5) EQUIVALENCE CONDUCTANCE:--

It is defined as"the conductance of a solution containing 1g equivalent of an electrolyte when placed between two sufficiently large electrodes which are 1 cm apart".

Equivalent conductance is denoted by λv,

where v = volume in cc containing 1 g equivalent of electrolyte dissolved in it and is measured in reciprocal ohms or mhos.

(6) MOLECULAR CONDUCTANCE:--

It is defined as "the conductance of a solution containing 1g mole of the electrolyte when placed between two sufficiently large electrodes placed 1 cm apart"

Molecular conductance is denoted by μ_v and it is measured in mhos.

(7) RELATION BETWEEN SPECIFIC CONDUCTANCE AND EQUIVALENT CONDUCTANCE:--

Let us consider a rectangular metallic vessel with opposite sides exactly 1 cm apart.

If 1 cc of the solution is now placed in this vessel, the areas of the opposite faces of the cube covered by the solution will be 1 sq cm.

Hence, measured conductance of the solution will be its specific condutence.

Or,

measured conductance = specific conductance--- --I

If 1 cc of the solution is placed in the above vessel containing 1 g equivalent of the electrolyte,

then the measured conductance will be equal to the equivalent conductance.

Or,

measured conductance = equivalent conductance------II

Hence,

from equation I and II,

we get equivalent conductance = specific conductance

Or, λ = k.

Now if 1 cc of this solution is diluted to 10cc by adding 9 cc of pure solvent

then measured conductance will still be equivalent conductance but it will be 10 times of the specific conductance.

Or,

λ = k x 10

If the solution is diluted 100 times its volume, then measured conductance will still be equivalent conductance.

But it will be 100 times the specific conductance.

Or,

λ = k x 100

If the solution containing 1 g equivalent of the electrolyte is dissolved in v cc of the solution,

then, λ = k x v

Hence,

$equivalent\ conductance = specific\ condutance \times volume\ of\ solution\ in\ c.c.$ containing 1 g equivalent of the electrolyte

(8) RELATION BETWEEN MOLECULAR CONDUCTANCE AND SPECIFIC CONDUCTANCE:--

It is similar to the relation between equivalent conductance and specific conductance.

Hence,

μ_v = k x v

Or,

molecular conductance = specific conductance x volume of solution containing 1g mole of the electrolyte

(9) KOHLRAUSCH'S LAW:--

It states that the equivalent conductivity of an electrolyte at infinite dilution is equal to the sum of the conductances of the anions and cations.

$$\lambda_{eq}^{\infty} = \lambda_c^{\infty} + \lambda_a^{\infty}$$

where λ_{eq}^{∞} = equivalent conductivity at infinite dilution.

λ_c^∞ = conductivity of cation at infinite dilution

λ_a^∞ = conductivity of anion at infinite dilution.

(10) CELL CONSTANT:--

It is known that observed conductivity is equal to specific conductivity when electrodes in cell are exactly one cm apart and have surface area of one sq cm. But it is not always true. Sometimes electrodes in the cell are not exactly one cm apart and may not have surface area of one sq cm. So, value of observed conductivity will not be equal to specific conductivity but proportional to it. Hence, it becomes important to calculate a factor for the conductivity cell, known as cell constant.

The cell constant when multiplied by the observed conductivity then it gives the value for specific conductivity.

As we know that,

$$R = \varrho \frac{L}{a}$$

Or,

$$R = \varrho x \ (where \ x = \frac{L}{a} = cell \ constant)$$

Or, $x = cell \ constant = \frac{R}{p} = \dfrac{\frac{1}{Observed \ conductivity}}{\frac{1}{Specific \ conductivity}}$

Or,

specific conductivity = cell constant x observed conductivity

For example,

Cell constant can be calculated by getting value of observed conductivity with the given cell by using N/50 KCl solution at 25°C and by determining specific conductivity for the value of 0.002765 mhos by using Kohlrausch law.

Or, $cell \ constant = \dfrac{specific \ conductivity}{observed \ conductivity}$

Or, $cell \ constant = \dfrac{0.002765}{observed \ conductivity}$

CONDUCTIVITY CELL:--

Conductivity cell is such type of cell where conductivity of the solution is measured by the use of electrodes, thermostat, resistant box with the supply of a source of atternative current.

Conductivity cell is a simple dipping cellwhich is made of pyrex glass or quartz and is fitted with platinum electrodes made of two parallel sheets of platinum foil as shown in Fig.8.

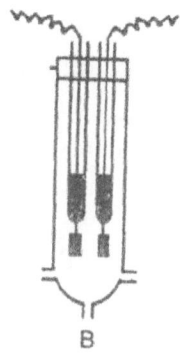

FIG.8 : Conductivity Cell

Relative position of electrodes are fixed by sealing the connected tubes into the side of the conductivity cell. Electrodes are coated with finely divided platinum black in order to remove polarization. The platinisation is carried out by taking 2 to 3% solution of chloroplatinic acid and 0.02 to 0.03 g of lead acetate in the cell. Further current can be passed for purpose of production of electrolysis of chloroplatinic acid by which electrodes get blackened due to coating of finely divided platinum.

MEASUREMENT OF CONDUCTANCE:--

APPARATUS:--

A modified form of the Wheatstone bridge is used as an apparatus for conductance measurement as shown in Fig.9.

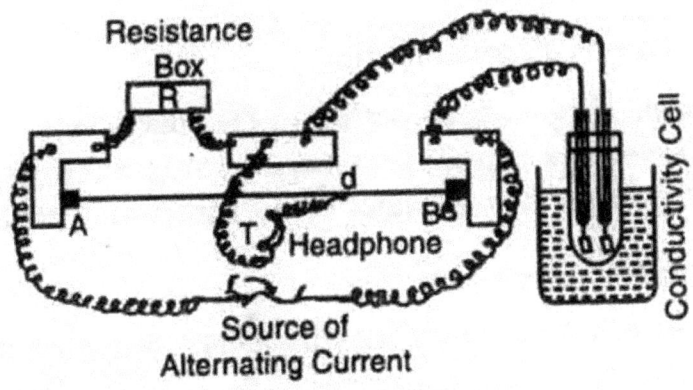

Fig.9 Wheatstone bridge

METHOD:--

At first solution, whose conductance is to be measured, is taken in the conducitivity cell. Then conducitivity cell is placed in the thermostat for maintenance of the temperature constant through out the experiment because conductance varies with the temperature. The conductivity cell is connected to a resistant box R on one side and to a long thin wire AB stretched along a scale on the other side. Then some known resistance 'R' is taken out of the reisistance box. An alternating current is passed through the solution with the help of an induction coil as a simple source of A.C. The sliding current d is moved on the wire AB so that minimum or no sound is heard in the head phone. Further conductivity of the solution can be calculated by the use of following relationship:--

$$\frac{Resistance\ of\ solution}{Resistance\ R} = \frac{Length\ Bd}{Length\ Ad}$$

By knowing R, Ad and Bd, the resistance of the solution can be calculated.

Since,

$$Counductivity\ of\ the\ solution = \frac{1}{Resistance\ of\ the\ solution}$$

So, by knowing resistance of the solution, the conductivity of the solution can be calculated.

APPLICATIONS OF CONDUCTANCE MEASUREMENT:--

(1) BASICITY OF ORGANIC ACIDS:--

With the help of following Ostwald's empirical relation, basicity of acid or sodium salt of organic acids can be calculated as such:--

$$B = \frac{\lambda_{1024} - \lambda_{32}}{10.8}$$

where λ_{1024} = equivalent conductance of salt at 25°C for dilutions of 1024 liters per g equivalent.

λ_{32} = equivalent conductance of salt at 25°C for dilutions of 32 liters per g equivalent.

and

B = Basicity of the acid.

METHOD:--

At first N/16 NaOH solution is prepared by dissolving 2.5g of NaOH in 1 liter of water in a volumetric flask. Then 100ml of N/16 solution is neutralized by adding a concentrated solution of the acid by using a suitable indicator. Further volume is made up to 100 ml after complete neutralization which gives N/32 solution of the salt. Then N/1024 solution can be prepared by accurate dilution of N/32 solution. After that equivalent conductivities of N/32 and N/1024 solution of the salt are measured. Finally basicity B of organic acids can be calculated by using above relation.

(2) SOLUBILITY OF SPARANGILY SOLUBLE SALTS:--

It is well known that the saturated solution of a sparingly soluble salt is so soluble that the electrolyte present in it can be considered as completely ionized.

A following relation can be given in between equivalent conductance (delta), the Specific conductance k and the Concentration C as such:--

$$delta = k \times \frac{1000}{C}$$

As solution is saturated, then C represents the solubility (in g equivalents per liter).

Example:--

Let us find out the solubility of AgCl (sparingly soluble salt) at 25°C.

At first soluble impurities present in AgCl is being removed by washing with conductivity water obtained by distilling distilled water. Further AgCl is suspended in conductivity water, warmed and kept at 25°C.

The obtained solution is known as saturated solution at 25°C. Further conductivity of solution is measured at 25°C by usual method. Value of equivalent conductance at particular dilution i.e., λv can be considered equal to equivalent conductance at infinite dilution, i.e., $\lambda \infty$.

So,

$\lambda v = \lambda \infty = Kv \times V$

where Kv = specific conductance at particular dilution

and V = volume of 1 g equivalent of the solute.

As per Kohlrausch's law,

$\lambda \infty = \lambda \infty (\text{cation}) + \lambda \infty (\text{anion})$

$= \lambda \infty (Ag^+) + \lambda \infty (cl^-)$

$= 61.92 + 76.35$

$= 138.27$

By knowing $\lambda \infty$ and Kv, the volume V can be determined.

Hence, Solubility s can be calculated.

As we know that,

Solubility, $S = \frac{1000}{V} \times E$ g/litre

where E = equivalent weight of the substance

Or,

$S = 1000 \times Ex \frac{Kv}{\lambda\infty}$ (because $V = \frac{\lambda\infty}{Kv}$)

$= \frac{1000 \times 143.5 \times Kv}{138.27}$ (as equivalent weight of $AgCl = 138.7$)

By knowing Kv, specific conductance, solubility of sparingly soluble salt, AgCl can be calculated.

(3) IONIC PRODUCT OF WATER:--

As we know that,

Ionic product of water = $[H^+][OH^-]$

Ionic product of water also can be calculated by knowing specific conductance and equivalent conductance at infinite dilution.

The equivalent conductance at infinite dilution, $\lambda\infty$ can be represented by following equation:--

$$\lambda\infty = \frac{K\infty}{C} \times 1000$$

where $K\infty$ = specific conductance at infinite dilution

and C = concentration of substance or water in g equivalent per liter

The experiment value of specific conductance of pure water is found to be 5.54×10^{-8} mhos cm-1 at 25°C. It can be regarded as a solution of ionized water at infinite dilution.

The value of equivalent conductances of the two ions of water at infinite dilution are $\lambda\infty(H^+) = 349.8$ mhos cm^2

$\lambda\infty (OH^-) = 198.6$ mhos cm^2

Hence,

$\lambda\infty (H_2O) = \lambda\infty(H^+) + \lambda\infty(OH^-)$

$= 349.8 + 198.6$

$= 548.4$ mhos cm^2

By substituting the values of $K\infty$ and $\lambda\infty$ in the equation,

$$\lambda\infty = \frac{K\infty}{C} \times 1000$$

we can get value of [H+] and [H-] concentrations.

Hence,
$$[H^+] = \frac{1000 \times K_\infty}{\lambda_\infty} = \frac{1000 \times 5.54 \times 10^{-8}}{5484}$$
$$= 1.01 \times 10^{-7}$$

and $[OH^+] = \frac{1000 \times K_\infty}{\lambda_\infty}$

$$= \frac{1000 \times 5.54 \times 10^{-8}}{548.4} = 1.01 \times 10^{-7}$$

Hence, Ionic product of water,
$$K_w = [H^+][OH^-]$$
$$= [1.01 \times 10^{-7}] \times [1.01 \times 10^{-7}]$$

= 1.02 X 10^{-14}

(4) DEGREE OF DISSOCIATION OF WEAKER ELECTROLYTES:--

Degree of dissociation of weaker electrolyte can be determined with the help of following equation:--

$$\propto = \frac{\lambda v}{\lambda \infty}$$

where λv = equivalent conductance at a given dilution v

and $\lambda\infty$ = equivalent conductance at infinite dilution.

$\lambda\infty$ can be obtained from equivalent conductance table and λv can be found experimentally. Hence, degree of dissociation of weak electrolyte can be calculated.

(5) DEGREE OF HYDROLYSIS:--

When a salt of weak acid or base is dissolved in water, then conductance of solution will be partly due to the ions of the salt and partly due to H$^+$ or OH$^-$ ions of the acid or base formed by hydrolysis. An excess of acid or base in the presence of its salt can be considered as completely unionized. Hence, the addition of weak acid or base to the salt solution suppresses the hydrolysis but ionization will be unaffected.

Let us consider a salt of weak base and strong acid i.e., aniline hydrochloride,

$C_6H_5NH_3 + Cl^- = C_6H_5NH_3^+Cl^-$

When aniline hydrochloride is hydrolysed then α equivalents of free acid and base are produced and (1 - α) equivalents of salt is not hydrolysed.

Here α is degree of hydrolysis.

It can be represented as such:--

$C_6H_5NH_3 \rightleftharpoons C_6H_5NH_2^+ + H^+$

(1 - α)   αα

The weak undissociated base aniline does not contribute to the total equivalent conductance, λ of this solution.

So, it can be represented as:--

$$\lambda = (1 - \lambda)_{\lambda c} + \alpha\, \lambda_{HCl}$$

Where λc = equivalent conductance of unhydrolysed salt.

λ_{HCl} = equivalent conductance of free acid

λc can be determined by measuring the equivalent conductance of $C_6H_5\,NH_3^+\,Cl^-$ in presence of excess of aniline.

The value of λ_{HCl} at concentrations of M/32, M/64 and M/128 are 393, 399 and 401

Thus, α can be calculated.

(6) DETERMINATION OF VANILLIN IN A VANILLA ESSENCE:--

Commercial vanilla essence contains about 1% of vanillin.

During the process of determination, at first 10 ml of essence is taken in a graduated cylinder and mixed with 40 ml of water containing 5g of common salt. Common salt helps in decreasing the miscibility of water and ether. Further contents are transferred into a separating funnel. Then 6N hydrochloric acid and 40- 60 ml of ether are added and shaken. After that ether layer is washed with distilled water then decanted into a beaker Finally it is evaporated on a steam bath. Then residue is dissolved in a mixture of 10 ml of ethyl alcohol and 75 ml of water and titrated conductometrically.

(7) CONDUCTOMETRIC TITRATIONS:--

Conductometric titration is such type of titration where end point of a titration is determined with the help of conductivity measurements.

Conductometric titration is carried out for such titrations where a sharp change in conductivity is obtained at the end point.

During the process of Conductometric titration, an electrolyte is added to a solution of another electrolyte under conditions that no change in volume should occur which may affect the conductance of the solution according to whether or not ionic reactions occur.

If no ionic reaction takes place, then conductance will simple rise with the addition of one simple salt to another.

For example, when potassium chloride is added to sodium nitrate.

But if ionic reactions occurs, then conductance may either increase or decrease.

For example, when a base is added to a strong acid, then conductance decreases due to replacement of the hydrogen ion of high conductivity by another cation of lower conductivity.

In other words, substitution of ions of one conductivity takes place by ions of another conductivity.

Let us see the change of conductance of a solution of a strong electrolyte A^+B^- when a reagent C^+D^- is added by assuming that the cation A^+ reacts with ion D^- of the reagent.

If the product of the reaction AD is relatively insoluble or only slightly ionized then reaction can be written as such

$$A^+B^- + C^+D^- = A^+D^- + C^+B^-$$

Hence, in the reaction between A^+ ions and D^- ions, the A^+ ions are replaced by C^+ ions during the titration.

As the titration proceeds, the conductance increases or decreases depending upon whether the conductivity of the C^+ ions is greater or less than A^+ ions.

In general, during the process of conductometric titration, a titration is added from the burette to a conductivity cell and subsequently conductvities are determined.

Futher values of conductivities are plotted against the volume of the titrant in c.c.

Since the measured conductivity is a linear function of the concentration of ions present, two ions may be obtained which may intersect each other at a point, known as end point or equivalence point.

When the reaction is not quantitative then some curvature may appear in the curve or in line near the end point which may be due to hydrolysis dissociation of the product or appreciable solubility in case of precipitations.In such cases the end point can be determined by extrapolating these portions of lines or curves.

It is known that conductivity of solution can be affected with the changes in temperature. The resistance decreases by about 1% to 2% for each degree increase in temperature. It is desirable to carry out measurement at constant temperature by using thermostat.

Further conductivity vessel and electrodes are thoroughly cleaned by immersion in a warm solution of potassium dichromate in concentrated sulphuric acid.After that it is washed with distilled water to make free from acid.Then electrodes are plated by the use of a mixture of solution of 3.0g chloroplatinic acid and 0.025g lead acetate per $100cm^3$

Further current is obtained from two accumulators (4 volts), then poles of which are connected to the ends of a suitable sliding resistance. The current is adjusted for production of a moderate evolution of hydrogen.

Each electrode should be used alternately as anode and cathode (i.e., the current should be reversed after every half minute) and electrolysis should be continued until both electrodes are covered with a jet-black deposit.

APPARATUS AND MEASUREMENTS:--

A conductivity cell is used for the determination of conductance required for conductometric titrations.

It is necessary to place the conductivity cell in a large vessel of water to maintain constancy of temperature. In most cases, the conductivity cell is used at the ambient temperature of the laboratory.

The conductivity cell should be of pyrex or other resistant glass and fitted with platinised platinum electrodes as platnising helps to minimize polarization effects. The size and separation of the electrodes is governed by the change of conductance during the titration. Electrodes should be large and close together for low conductance solution. Electrodes must be vertical for precipitation titrations. The electrodes are made free from traces of chlorine after platinising. Dilute sulphric acid is electrolysed during 15 minutes by using two platinised electrodes as cathode and another platinum electrode as anode. Further electrodes are washed with distilled water and kept immersed in distilled water until required for use.

A suitable cell for conductometric titration is depicted in below Fig.10

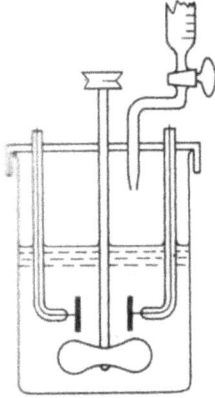

Fig.10: A SUITABLE CELL FOR CONDUCTOMETRIC TITRATION

The conductivity cell consists of a dipping electrodes which are firmly fixed in the Perspex lid and provided with a beaker of the suitable size along with openings for the mechanical stirring device and the jet of burette.The conductance measurements are made by using a Wheatstone bridge circuit (as already discussed under the method of conductance measurement).

In order to get straight line graphs it is essential that the total volume of the solutions should be constant during the titration. The concentration of the titrant should be 10 times as the solution being titrated to keep the volume change to small extent.

A correction to the reading can be applied whenever it is found necessary.

So, $Actual\ conductivity = \left(\frac{\vartheta+V}{V}\right) \times observed\ conductivity$

where v = volume of the titrant or reagent added

V = Initial volume

$\vartheta + V$ = Final volume

The correction presupposes that conductivity is a linear function of the dilution.

TYPES OF CONDUCTOMETRIC TITRATIONS:--

Or,

APPLICATION OF CONDUCTOMETRIC TITRATION:--

(a) ACID BASE TITRATIONS:--

(i) STRONG ACID WITH A STRONG BASE:--

Let us consider the titration of a strong acid like HCl with a strong base like NaOH.

The acid is taken in a conductivity vessel and the alkali in the burette.The conductance of hydrochloric acid is due to the presence of hydrogen and chloride ion.When NaOH is added to HCl, then high mobile hydrogen ions are replaced by less mobile sodium ions.

It can be represented as such:--

$$[H^+ + Cl^-] + [Na^+ + OH^-] \rightarrow [Na^+ + Cl^-] + H_2O$$

On continued addition of sodium hydroxide, the conductance decreases until the acid gets completely neutralized.The solution at neutralization i.e, at the end point containing only sodium and chloride ions have a minimum conductivity.Now if more NaOH is added then conductivity increases due to fast moving hydroxyl ions in compare to Na^+ ions.

Hence, if the titration is carried out at constant temperature and conductivity is plotted against the volume of sodium hydroxide added. Then the point of intersection of the two lines gives the end point as shown in Fig11.

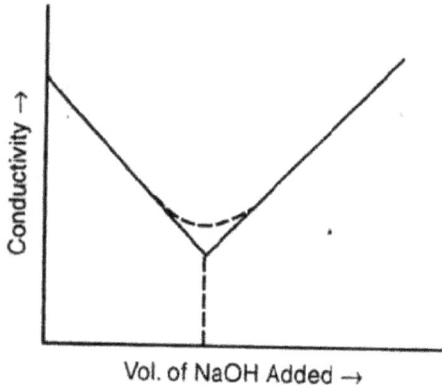

Fig.11. Titration of a strong acid with a strong base

In actual practice the lines may be slightly curved because of (i) variation in temperature due to heat of neutralization (ii) inter ionic effect and (iii) increase in the volume of solution because of the addition of the reagent.

Inspite of these, the inflection is sharp enough to get the exact end point.

(ii) STRONG ACID WITH A WEAK BASE:--

Let us consider the titration of strong acid like HCl acid with weak base like NH_4OH. When ammonium hydroxide is added to hydrochloric acid, then conductivity decreases due to replacement of fast moving H^+ ions by slow moving NH_4^+ ions

$$[H^+ + Cl^-] + [NH_4^+ + OH^-] \rightarrow [NH_4^+ + Cl^-] + H_2O$$

The addition of NH_4OH after end point does not change the conductance because NH_4OH is a weakly ionized electrolyte and it has a very small conductivity in compare to acid or its salt. It is shown in Fig.12.

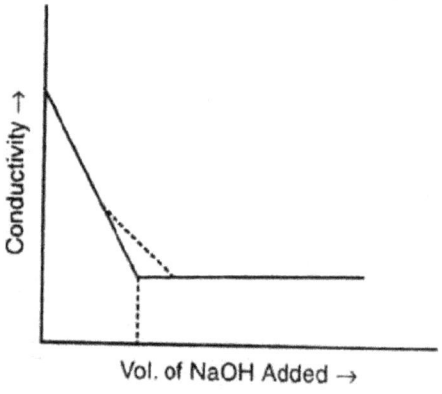

Fig.12. Titration of a strong acid with weak base

(iii) **WEAK ACID WITH A STRONG BASE:-**

Let us consider the titration of weak acid like CH_3COOH with strong base like NaOH.

When a small amount of NaOH is added to CH_3COOH, the conductivity decreases initially and then increases with further addition of NaOH.

$$[CH_3COO^- + H^+] + [Na^+ + OH^-] \rightarrow [CH_3COO^- + Na^+] + H_2O$$

After completion of neutralization of the acid, NaOH is added and it produces excess of OH⁻ ions by which conductance of solution increases more as shown in below Fig.13

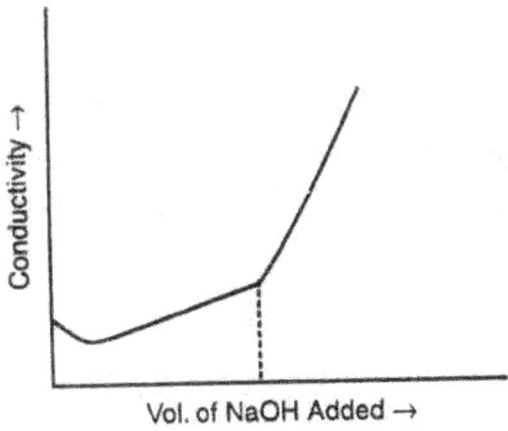

Fig.13.Titration of a weak acid with astrong base

(iv) **WEAK ACID WITH A WEAK BASE:--**

When a weak base like NH4OH is added to weak acid like CH3COOH then neutralization curve is obtained as shown in Figure 14

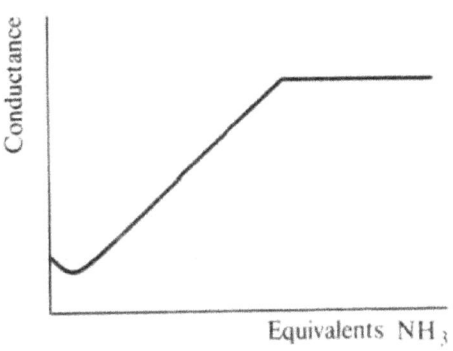

Fig.14.Titration of a weak acid with a weak base

$$[CH_3COO^- + H^+] + [NH_4^+ + OH^-] \rightarrow [CH_3COO^- + NH_4^+] + H_2O$$

The neutralization curve up to the equivalence point is similar to that obtained with sodium hydroxide solution, since both ammonium and sodium acetates are strong electrolytes. But after the equivalence point an excess of aqueous ammonia solution has little effect upon the conductivity, as its dissociation is depressed by the ammonium salt present in the solution.

(v) MIXTURE OF A STRONG ACID AND A WEAK ACID WITH A STRONG BASE:--

When a strong base like NaOH is added to a mixture of a strong acid, HCl and weak acid, CH_3COOH then conductance falls until the strong acid is neutralized. Further it rises as the weak acid is converted into its salt and finally rises more steeply as excess of alkali is introduced. Such a titration curve is shown as S in Fig 15

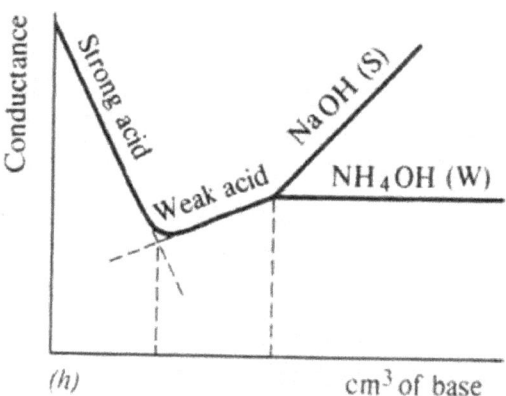

Fig.15. Titration of a strong acid and weak acid with a strong base

The three branches of the curve will be straight line except in so far as

(a) Increasing dissociation of the weak acid results in a rounding off at the first end point and (b) Hydrolysis of the salt of the weak acid causes a rounding off at the second end point.

Usually, extrapolation of the straight portions of the three branches lead to definite location of the end point. The curve w in diagram is obtained by substituting aqueous ammonia solution for the strong alkali. This procedure is generally applied for the determination of mineral acid in vinegar.

(b) DISPLACEMENT OR (REPLACEMENT) TITRATIONS:--

When a strong acid like HCl acid reacts with sodium or potassium salts of weak acids like CH_3COONa then weaker acid replaces first as such

$$[CH_3COO^- + Na^+] + [H + Cl^-] \rightarrow [CH_3COO^- + H^+] + [Na^+ + Cl^-]$$

In this titration only a slight increase in conductance is obtained upto end point because chloride ion has higher conductance than the acetate ion. After the end point, it increases more rapidly, owing to the addition of excess of hydrochloric acid as shown in figure 16.

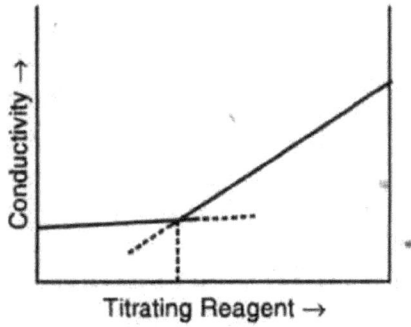

Fig.16: DISPLACEMENT TITRATION

The end point can be determined by the interaction of two lines.

Replacement titration is also seen during the titration of strong acid (NH_4Cl) with NaOH

$$[NH_4^+ + Cl^-] + [Na^+ + OH^-] \rightarrow [NH_4^+ + OH^-] + [Na^+ + Cl^-]$$

The main application of replacement titration is in the determination of alkaloids.

(C) PRECIPITATION TITRATION:--

When silver nitrate is added to the solution of potassium chloride, then precipitation reaction occurs with the formation of precipitate of AgCl.

$$[K^+ + Cl^-] + [Ag^+ + NO_3^-] \rightarrow [AgCl] + [K^+ + NO_3^-]$$

Conductance does not change much in the initial stage of the titration with the addition of silver nitrate because Cl⁻ ions are replaced by NO_3^- ions and both have almost same ionic conductance. After the end point, the excess of silver nitrate added causes a sharp increase in the conductance. Hence end point of the titration can be determined as shown in **Figure 17.**

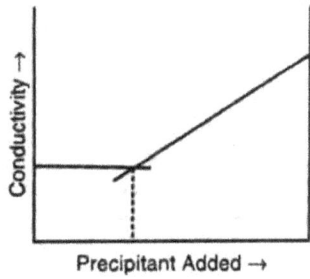

Fig.17: PRECIPITATION TITRATION

(D) REDOX TITRATIONS:--

When solution of potassium dichromate is added to the solution of ferrous sulphate in the presence of dilute H_2SO_4 acid then ferrous sulphate oxidizes into ferric sulphate where as potassium dichromate reduces into chromium sulphate as shown in following ionic equation.

$$6Fe^{2+} + Cr_2O_7^{2-} + 14H^+ \rightarrow 6Fe^{3+} + 2Cr^{3+} + 7H_2O$$

Here a sharp decrease in the conductance is observed upto the equivalence point due to high mobility of hydrogen ions during the initial part of redox titration as shown in Fig.18 The fraction of hydrogen ion removed is relatively small. Hence entire change in conductance is not great and can not be detected with accuracy by the usual equipment used for conductometric titrations.

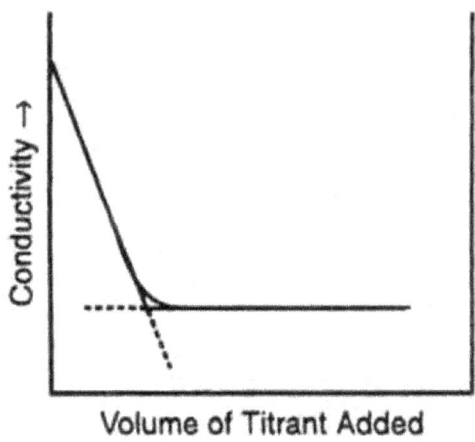

Fig.18 : REDOX TITRATION

(E) COMPLEXOMETRIC TITRATIONS:--

When solution of mercuric perchlorate is added to the solution of potassium chloride then mercuric chloride ion is formed and further when mercuric chloride reacts with potassium ions then potassium mercuric iodide is obtained.Hence two breaks are obtained during the titration of KCl with $Hg(ClO_4)_2$.The first break is due to the formation of $HgCl_2^{2-}$ and the second break is at the completion of reaction due to formation of K_2HgCl_4.

These reactions can be represented as such:--

$$Hg(ClO_4)_2 + 4KCl \rightarrow HgCl_4^{2-} + 2K^+ + 2KClO_4$$

$$HgCl_4^{2-} + 2K^+ \rightarrow K_2HgCl_4$$

(e) Conductance measurement is used for the determination of atmospheric sulphur dioxide.

(f) Conductometric titration is also used for the measurement of salinity of sea water in oceanographic work.

ADVANTAGES OF CONDUCTOMETRIC TITRATIOS:--

i)   Conductometric titrations are used for analysis of very weak acids and of dilute solutions.

ii)   Conductometric titration can be used in case of coloured liquids where normal indicators can not work.

iii)   It is useful for the measurement of approximate conductance of the solution.

DISADVANTAGE OF CONDUCTOMETRIC TITRATIONS:--

(i)It is not so useful for the measurement of conductance in redox titrations because substantial excess of hydronium ion needed for reactions tends to mask conductivity changes.

(ii)It is less accurate and satisfactory with increasing total electrolytic concentration. Actually the change in conductance due to the addition of titrant can become largely masked by high salt concentrations in the solution being titrated. So under these circumstances, the method can not be used.

(b)POTENTIOMETRY

Or,

POTENTIOMETRIC TITRATION:--

Potentiometric titration is such type of titration by which quantity of unknown substance can be determined by the help of known quantity of titrant until the entire unknown substance consumes for titration.

After the titration method, the potential difference is measured in between the two electrodes i.e, reference and indicator electrode in conditions where thermodynamic equilibrium is maintained and current passing through electrodes should not disturb the equilibrium.

Potentiometric titration is used to determine the concentration of a given analyte or unknown substance. It is used in characterization of the acids. No any chemical indicator is used in potentiometric titration. Instead to this, electric potential is measured across the substance.

In potentiometric titration generally an electrochemical cell is used with a reference electrode, salt bridge, analyte and an indicator electrode.Generally, electrolyte solution is used as analyte.

Hydrogen electrode, silver chloride electrode and calomel electrode are used as reference electrodes whereas glass electrode and metal ion electrode are used as indicator electrode.

REFERENCE ELECTRODE is such type of electrode which maintains its potential and remains stable when dipped into a sample solution.

INDICATOR ELECTRODE is such type of electrode which responds to variation in the potential of unknown solution.

A salt bridge is used to prevent interference of the analyte with the reference electrode.

The electromotive force or overall potential difference can be calculated by using following formula:--

$E_{cell} = E_{ind} - E_{ref} + E_j$

where E_{cell} = electromotive force or overall potential

E_{ind} = electromotive force of indicator electrode

E_{ref} = electromotive force of reference electrode

E_j = electromotive force at the junction across the salt bridge.

The electrode potential of the cell is dependent on the concentration of ions in contact with the indicator electrode. As a result E cell is measured after each addition.

Potentiometric titration involves the measurement of the potential of an indicator electrode with respect to a reference electrode as a function of titrant volume.

In potentiometric titration, the cell potential is measured and recorded in millivolts or pH after adding titrant each time when end point is approached then addition of titrant is stated in very small quantities.

The endpoint is detected by plotting a graph between cell potential on y axis and volume of titrant on x axis. The midpoint of the steeply rising portion of the graph or curve is estimated visually and taken as an endpoint as shown in Fig 19

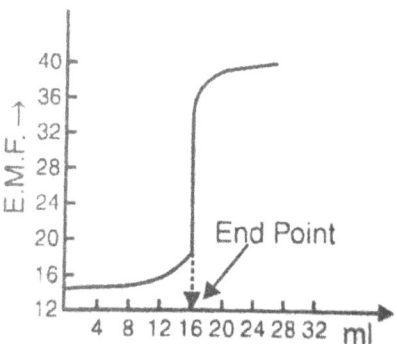

Fig19: Potentiometry titration

ELECTROCHEMICAL CELL:--

It is a device which can generate electrical energy from the chemical reactions occurring in it or use the electrical energy supplied to it to facilitate chemical reactions in it.

It has an capacity to convert chemical energy into electrical energy or vice versa.

Example:- Standard 1.5 volt cell is used to power electrical appliance like TV remotes and clocks.Electrochemical cell generally consists of a cathode and an anode.Cathode is denoted by a positive sign since electrons are consumed here whereas anode is denoted by a negative sign since electrons are liberated here.A reduction reaction occurs in the cathode of an electrochemical cell whereas an oxidation reaction occurs in the anode of an electrochemical cell.Electrons move into the cathode whereas electrons move out of the anode.General convention states that the cathode should be represented on the right-hand side whereas anode is represented on the left-hand side while denoting an electochemical cell.

Electro chemical cell is of two types:--

(1) GALVANIC CELL OR VOLTAIC CELL

(2) ELECTROLYTIC CELL

(1) GALVANIC CELL:--

Chemical energy is transformed into electrical energy and redox reactions take place which are spontaneous in nature.Anode is negatively charged whereas cathode is positively charged. Electrons originate from the species that undergo oxidation.

(2) ELECTROLYTIC CELL:--

Electrical energy is transformed into chemical energy in these cells.An input of energy is required for the redox reactions to proceed in these cells i.e, the reactions are non-spontaneous. These cells consist a positively charged anode and a negatively charged cathode. Electrons orginate from an external source (such as a battery).

APPLICATIONS OF ELECTROCHEMICAL CELL:--

Electrochemical cell is used in the process of electro refining and electro winning of non-ferrous metals.It is used for production of high-purity lead, zinc, aluminium and copper.

Metallic sodium can be extracted from molten sodium chloride by placing it in an electrolytic cell and passing an electric current through it.It is used to make lead-acid battery.Fuel cell class of electrochemical cell is used as a source of clean energy in several remote locations.

CONSTRUCTION AND WORKING OF REFERENCE AND INDICATOR ELECTRODE :--

(A) REFERENCE ELECTRODE:--

(1) STANDARD HYDROGEN ELECTRODE:--

Standard hydrogen electrode consists of a piece of platinum foil, coated electrolytically with platinum black and immersed in a solution of hydrochloric acid containing hydrogen ions at unit activity. (It corresponds to 1.8M-hydrochloric acid at 25°C)

Hydrogen gas at a pressure of one atmosphere is passed over the platinum foil through the side tube as shown in below Fig-20

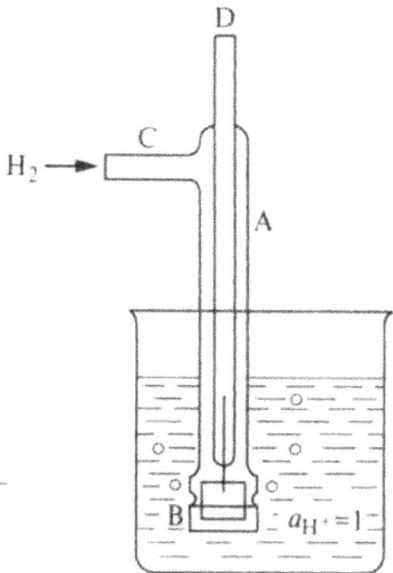

Fig.20:--Standard hydrogen electrode

and escapes through the small holes B in the surrounding glass tube A. Due to periodic formation of bubbles, the level of the liquid inside the tube fluctuates and a part of the foil is alternatively exposed to the solution and to hydrogen. The lower end of the foil is continuously immersed in the solution to avoid interruption of the electric current. Connection between the platinum foil and an external circuit is made with mercury in D.

The platinum black has the remarkable property of adsorbing large quantities of hydrogen and it permits the change from the gaseous to the ionic form and reverse process to occur without hindrance; so it behaves as though it were composed entirely of hydrogen, i.e., as a hydrogen electrode.

Under fixed conditions, for example hydrogen gas at atmospheric pressure and unit activity of hydrogen ions in the solution in contact with the electrode, the hydrogen electrode possesses a definite potential.

By convention, the potential of the standard hydrogen electrode is equal to zero at all temperatures.

Upon connecting the standard hydrogen electrode with a metal electrode (a metal in contact with a solution of its ions of unit activity) by means of a salt bridge (eg. Potassium chloride), the standard electrode potential can be determined.

The cell is usually written as:--

Pt, $H_2|H^+$ (a = 1) $\parallel M^{n+}$ (a=1) | M

where, Single vertical line represents a metal-electrolyte boundary at which a potential difference is taken into account and a double vertical line represents a liquid junction at which the potential is considered to be eliminated by a salt bridge.

When we speak of the electrode potential of a zinc chloride, we mean the e.m.f of the cell:--

Pt, $H_2| H^+$ (a=1) $\parallel Zn^{2+}$ | Zn

Or,

the e.m.f of the half-cell Zn^{2+} | Zn

The cell reaction is:--

$H_2 + Zn^{2+} = 2H^+$ (a=1) + Zn

and the half-cell reaction is written as

$Zn^{2+} +2e \rightleftharpoons Zn$

The convention is adopted of writing half-cell reactions as reduction

$M^{n+} +ne \rightleftharpoons M$

For example,

$Zn^{2+} + 2e \rightleftharpoons Zn$, E^θ = - 0.76 volt

When the activity of the ion M^+ is equal to unity (approximately for a 1M solution)

then electrode potential E becomes equal to the standard potential E^θ.

The Standard electrode potential is a quantitative measure of the readiness of element as a reducing agent in aqueous solution; the more negative the potential of the element, the more powerful is its action as a reductant.

For example, Standard electrode potentials at 25°C of electrode reaction can be summerised as such ---

			E^θ volts
1.	$Ca^{2+} + 2e = Ca$	-	2.87
2.	$Al^{3+} + 3e = Al$	-	1.66
3.	$Fe^{2+} + 2e = Fe$	-	0.440
4.	$Ni^{2+} + 2e \rightleftharpoons Ni$	-	0.25
5.	$Ag^+ + e = Ag$	+	0.799

STANDARD HYDROGEN ELECTRODE:--

Standard electrode potential of standard hydrogen electrode is declared to be 0(zero) at a temperature of 298K.

This is bsecuase it acts as a reference for comparision with any other electrode. The half reaction of standard hydrogen electrode can be written as follows:--

$2H^+ (aq) + 2e^- \rightarrow H_2 (g)$

The reaction given above generally takes place on a platinum electrode.

The pressure of the hydrogen gas present in this half cell equals 1 bar.

ELECTRODE POTENTIALS:--

When a metal is immersed in a solution containing its own ions, e.g. zinc in zinc sulphate solution, a potential difference or electrode potential is established between the metal and the solution.

The potential difference or electrode potential E for an electrode reaction can be written as:--

$M^{n+} + ne \rightleftharpoons M$

It is given by the expression:--

$$E = E^\theta + \frac{RT}{nF} \ln a_M n^+ \quad \text{---------- I}$$

Where,

R = gas constant

= 8.3144598 J Mol^{-1}K^{-1} (Joule per Kelvin per mole)

T = absolute temperature = 298K

F = Faraday constant = 96485.33289 Cmol^{-1} (coulomb per mole)

n = Valency of the ions

a_M^{n+} = the activity of ions

E^θ = Standard electrode potential of the metal.

Equation (I) can be simplified by introducing the known values of R and F and converting by 2.3026, then it becomes

$$E = E^\theta + \frac{0.0001983T}{n} \log a_M^{n+}$$

For a temperature of 25°C (T = 298K)

$$E = E^\theta + \frac{0.0591}{n} \log a_M^{n+} \quad \text{----- (II)}$$

For most purposes in quantitative analysis, it is sufficiently accurate to replace a_M^{n+} by C_M^{n+}, the ion concentration (in moles per dm³)

$$E = E^\theta + \frac{0.0591}{n} \log C_M^{n+} \quad \text{----- (III)}$$

This equation is a form of Nernst equation.

If in equation (II), a_M^{n+} is put equal to unity, then E is equal to E^θ.

E^θ is called the standard electrode potential.

It is necessary to have another electrode and solution accurately known potential difference in order to determine the potential difference between an electrode and a solution. Further two electrodes can be combined to form a voltaic cell, the e.m.f of which can be directly measured.

The e.m.f of the cell is the arithmetical sum or difference of the electrode potentials (depending upon the sign of these two potentials). Further the value of the unknown potential can be calculated.

The primary reference electrode is the normal or standard hydrogen electrode.

(2) THE CALOMEL ELECTRODE:--

The calomel electrode is widely used as reference electrode due to its ease of preparation and constancy of potential.

A calomel half-cell is one in which mercury and calomel [[mercury (I) chloride] are covered with potassium chloride solution of definite concentration. It may be 0.1N, 1.0N, 3.5N or saturated. The potassium chloride solution must be saturated with the calomel. The potentials of the 0.1N, 1.0N and saturated calomel electrodes at 25°C relative to the normal hydrogen electrode are 0.3371, 0.2846 and 0.2458 volt respectively.

APPARATUS:--

The calomel electrode consists of a glass vessel provided with a bent side tube A and another side tube B, over the end of which a piece of rubber tubing is placed which can be closed by a spring or screw clip as shown in Fig.21.

An electrical connection is made with electrode by means of a platinum wire which is sealed through a glass tube C. Glass tube C contains a little pure mercury into which an amalgamated copper wire dips. A saturated solution of analytically pure potassium chloride containing some of the solid salt is prepared for purpose of setting up the electrode. Further pure mercury to a depth of 0.5-1 cm is placed in the bottom of the dry electrode vessel. Then mercury is covered with a large of calomel paste D.

Calomel paste D is prepared by rubbing pure calomel, mercury and saturated potassium chloride solution together in a glass mortar. Then supernatant liquid is poured off and the rubbing process is repeated twice with fresh quantities of saturated potassium chloride solution. The rubber bung carrying the glass tube and platinum wire is inserted. A care is taken that the platinum wire dips into the mercury. The vessel is filled with a saturated solution of potassium chloride (previously saturated with calomel by shaking with the solid salt) by drawing in the solution through the bent tube A and then closing the rubber tube B with a clip.

The electrode is then ready for use.

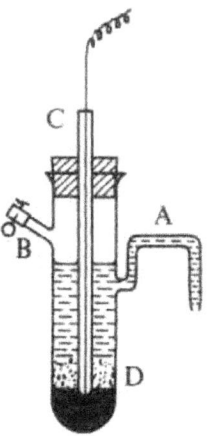

Fig. 21. THE CALOMEL ELECTRODE

(3) THE SILVER-SILVER CHLORIDE ELECTRODE:- It consists of a silver wire or a silver-plated platinum wire, coated electrolytically with a thin layer of silver chloride, dipping into a potassium chloride solution of known concentration. The potentials of the 0.1M and saturated silver-silver chloride electrode at 25°C with respect to the normal (or standard) hydrogen electrode are 0.290 and 0.199 volt resspectively.

Silver – silver chloride electrode is commonly used as reference electrode for testing cathodic protection corrosion control systems in sea water environments.

The electrode functions as a reversible redox electrode and the equilibrium in between the solid silver metal (Ag) and its solid salt-silver chloride (AgCl) also called silver (1) chloride in a chloride solution of a given concentration.

In electro chemical cell notation, the silver chloride electrode is written as example for an electrolyte solution of KCl 3M; Ag/AgCl/KCl (3M)

The corresponding half reactions can be presented as follows:--

$$Ag^+ + e^- \rightleftharpoons Ag$$

$$AgCl(s) + e^- \rightleftharpoons Ag(s) + Cl^-$$

Or,

It can be written together as such:--

$$AgCl + Ag(s) + e^- \rightleftharpoons Ag(s) + e^- + Cl^- + Ag^+$$

which can be simplified

$$AgCl(s) \rightleftharpoons Ag^+ + Cl^-$$

This reaction is a reversible reaction and is characterized by fast electrode kinetics, meaning that a sufficiently high current can be passed through the electrode with 100% efficiency of the redox reaction (anodic oxidation and dissolution of Ag metal along with cathodic reduction and deposition of the Ag^+ ions as Ag metal on the surface of the Ag wire)

The reaction has been proven to obey these equations in solutions of pH values between 0 and 13.5.

The Nernst equation below shows the dependence of the potential of the silver- silver (1) chloride on the activity or effective concentration of chloride ions

$$E = E^\theta - \frac{RT}{F}|NaCl^-$$

The standard electrode potential E^θ against standard hydrogen electrode is 0.230V±10mv.

sto the normal (or standard) hydrogen electrode are 0.290 and 0.199 volt resspectively.

(B) INDICATOR ELECTRODE:--

Indicator electrode of a cell is one whose potential is dependent upon the activity (or, the concentration) of a particular ionic species whose concentration is to be determined.

A simple indicator electrode usually consists of a carefully cleaned rod or wire of the appropriate metal in case of direct potentiometry or potentiometric titration of a metal ion. When hydrogen ions are involved, a hydrogen electrode can be used as indicator electrode.

(1)THE METAL ELECTRODE

Or,

THE ANTIMONY ELECTRODE:--

The antimony electrode is actually an antimony-antimony trioxide electrode. The electrode is usually prepared by casting a stick of antimony in the presence of air. Sufficient oxidation occurs in this way to facilitate further addition of oxide unnecessary. A wire attached to one end of the antimony rod while the other end is inserted into the experimental solution. Then potential is measured against a convenient reference electrode. As the potentials differ from one electrode to another electrode, so it becomes necessary to standardise each antimony electrode by means of solutions of known pH and also under the same experimental condition to which it may be subjected in use.

For example, in the presence or absence of oxygen.

The most useful pH range is 2-8.

The antimony electrode can not be applied in the following cases:--

(1) In the presence of strong oxidizing agents or of complexing agents e.g as tartrates and organic hydroxyl acids.

(II)In solutions with a pH lower than 3.

(III)In the presence of the metals more soluble than antimony.

The electrode is not readily poisoned, is simple to use and is rugged. So it has application for the continuous recording or control of pH in conditions where it is applicable.

The following electrode reaction can be discussed in case of antimony electrode:--

$Sb_2O_3 + 6H^+ + 6e \rightleftharpoons 2Sb + 3H_2O$

and the potential at 25°C is theoretically given by

$$E = E^\theta Sb_2O_3, Sb \frac{0.0591}{6} \log \frac{1}{a^6 H^+} = E^\theta Sb_2O_3, Sb - 0.0591\, pH$$

The activity of the solid antimony, antimony trioxide and of the water, being taken as unity.

In practice, it is found that the pH response of the Sb, Sb_2O_3 electrode is roughly given by above equation but exact limits of the validity of this relation are uncertain.

(2) THE GLASS ELECTRODE:--

The glass electrode is widely used hydrogen-ion responsive electrode and its use is dependent upon the fact that when a glass membrane is immersed in a solution, a potential is developed which is a linear function of the hydrogen ion concentration of the solution. The glass electrode consists of a bulb which is immersed in the solution of which it is required to measure the hydrogen ions concentration and the electric circuit is completed by filling the bulb with a solution of .1M hydrochloric acid and inserting a silver-silver chloride electrode.

If internal hydrochloric acid is maintained at constant concentration, then potential of the silver-silver chloride electrode inserted into it remains constant and same potential remains in between the hydrochloric acid solution and the inner surface of the glass bulb.

So, only potential varies in between the outer surface of the glass bulb and the test solution into which it is immersed.

Like this overall potential of the electrode is governed by the hydrogen ion concentration of the test solution.

The upper end of the electrode must be sealed for purpose of maintaining concentration of the inner hydrochloric acid solution to remain constant.

Such type of electrode is shown in Fig 22.

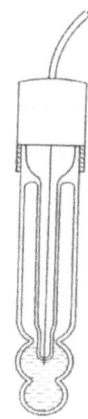

Fig.22 : Glass bulb

Glass used for construction of glass electrode should have following composition:--

SiO_2, 63%; Li_2O, 28%; La_2O_3, 3%

Such composition has an error of only -0.12pH at pH 12.8 in the presence of sodium ions at a concentration of 2M.

Glass electrode should be combined with a reference electrode for measuring the hydrogen ion concentration of a solution. So saturated calomel electrode is commonly used for such purpose and it gives the cell as such:--

Ag , AgCl / HCl (0.1M) glass / Test solution || KCl (Sat'd), Hg_2Cl_2 / Hg.

A specialized instrument can be used for measuring the cell e.m.f.

The e.m.f of the cell can be expressed by the use of following equation:--

$$E = K + (RT/F) \ln a_{H^+}$$

Or,

at a temperature of 25°C by the expression

E = K + 0.0591 pH

Where K = constant partly dependent upon the nature of the glass used in the construction of the membrane and partly upon the individual character of each electrode; Its value may vary slightly with time.

Glass electrodes require soaking in water for some hours before use. Subsequently a hydrated layer is formed on the glass surface, inside which an ions exchange process can take place.

If the glass contains sodium, the exchange process can be represented by the equilibrium:--

$$H^+_{soln} + Na^+_{glass} \rightleftharpoons H^+_{glass} + Na^+_{soln}$$

The concentration of the solution within the glass bulb is fixed and hence on the inner side of the bulb an equilibrium condition leading to a constant potential is established.

On the outside of the bulb, the potential developed will be dependent upon the hydrogen ion concentration of the solution in which the bulb is immersed. The glass electrode can be used in the presence of strong oxidants and reductants in different media and in presence of proteins which seriously interfere with other electrodes. The glass electrode should be thoroughly washed with distilled water after each measurement and then rinsed with several portions of the next test solution before making the following measurement.

The glass electrode should not be allowed to become dry except during long periods of storage. It may return to its responsive condition when immersed in distilled water for at least twelve hours prior to use.

METHOD TO DETERMINEEND POINT IN POTENTIOMETRIC TITRATION:--

During the process of determination of end point in potentiometric titration, at first solution of unknown substance is taken in a beaker (as shown in figure 23). Then a reference electrode A (eg. A saturated calomel half cell), an indicator electrode B and mechanical stirrer or (magnetic stirrer) are placed in position as shown in figure23.

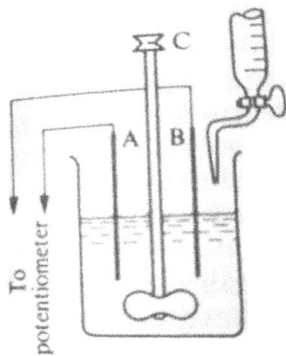

Fig.23. Apparatus used for Potentiometric titration

After that basic or other solutions free from atmospheric CO_2 is added by using large increments like 1-5 cm^3.

Subsequently e.m.f of the cell containing initial solution is determined and addition of titrant is continued until the equivalence point is reached. The e.m.f is determined after each addition. Sufficient time should be allowed after each addition for the indicator electrode to reach a reasonably constant potential (to ± 1-2 millivolts) before points should be obtained well beyond the equivalence point .Electrode system should be connected to a potentiometer or millivoltmeter for the purpose of measuring e.m.f and recording the results of different types of potentiometric titrations as well as for getting of continuous record of the titration results or titration curves.

LOCATION OF END POINTS:--

A titration curve is obtained by plotting e.m.f. readings against volume of titrant added either by manual plotting of the experimental readings or with suitable equipment plotted automatically during the course of titration.

The central portion of such a curve is shown in Fig 24 and also in Fig 25

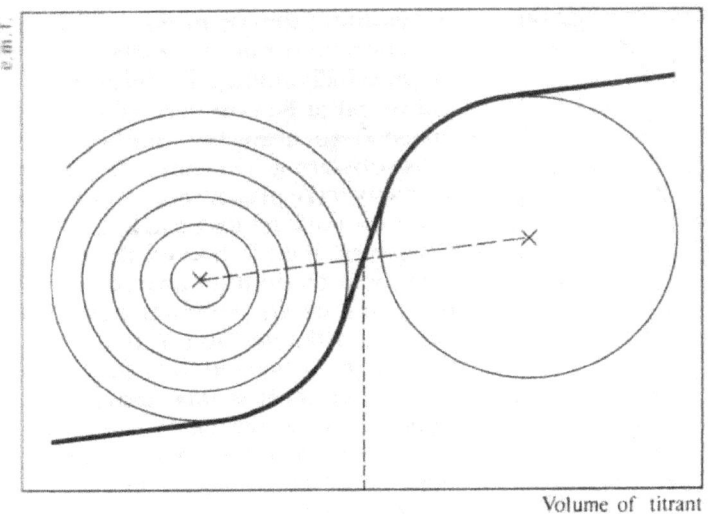

Fig.24

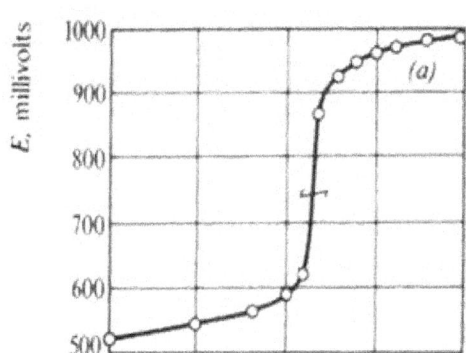

Fig.25. LOCATION OF END POINT IN POTENTIOMETRY

and clearly the end point can be located on the steeply rising portion of the curve and it occurs at the point of inflection.

In general end point can be located by the use of the method of bisection for such curve when it shows reasonably good straight lines before and after the steep part of the curve.

Each of these straight lines is extended (the lower portion to the right, the upper portion to the half) and then at suitable points vertical lines are erected, one to the right of the steep part of the titration curve and one to the left. These vertical lines are then bisected and the midpoints are joined; where the line joining the midpoints cuts the titration curve is the end point of the titration.

End point of the titration can be obtained accurately by the use of analytical or derivative methods.

By this method first derivative curve ($\Delta E / \Delta V$ against V) or second derivative curve ($\Delta^2 E / \Delta V^2$ against V) can be plotted. The first derivative curve gives a maximum at the point of inflection of the titration curve i.e. at the end point whereas the second derivative ($\Delta^2 E/\Delta V^2$) is zero at the point where the slope to the ($\Delta E/\Delta V$) curve is maximum.

Further the same can be explained by taking example of potentiometric titration of 25cm³ of 0.1M ammonium iron (II) sulphate with standard 0.1095M cerium (IV) sulphate solution using platinum and saturated calomel electrode.

$$Fe^{2+} + Ce^{4+} \rightleftharpoons Fe^{3+} + Ce^{3+}$$

Some results are described in below table:--

Table – 4: Potentiometric titration of Fe^{2+} solution with 0.1095 M-Ce^{4+} solution using platinum and calomel electrode

Ce^{4+} solution added, cm³(V)	Em(V)	$\Delta E/\Delta V$ (mV/cm³)	$\Delta^2 E/\Delta V^2$
1.00	373	10.5	
5.00	415	4.6	0
10.00	438	4.2	100
15.00	459	6.4	200
20.00	491	12	500
21.00	503	20	1500
22.00	523	40	21000
22.50	543	70	-18500
22.60	550	70	-2600
22.70	557	80	-1500
22.80	565	100	-840
			-300

22.90	575	150	-90
23.00	590	300	
23.10	620	2400	
23.20	860	550	
23.30	915	290	
23.40	944	140	
23.50	958	56	
24.00	986	40.5	
26.00	1067	14.5	
30.00	1125		

By observing the same above table, it is clear that only experimental figures in the vicinity of the equivalence point are required to locate the end point.

The below figure 25can be described as such

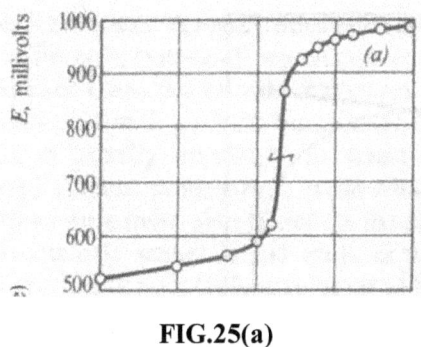

FIG.25(a)

Fig25(a):-- It represents the part of the experimental titration curve in the vicinity of the equivalence point.

Fig25(b):-- The slope of the titration curve as a function of V (the equivalence point is indicated by the maximum which corresponds to the inflexion in the titration curve) and

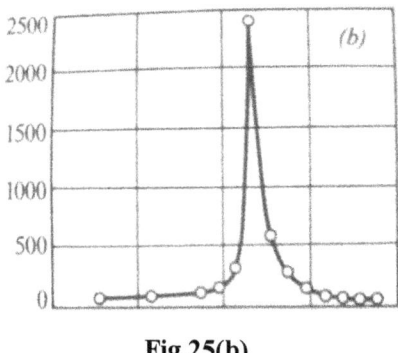

Fig.25(b)

Fig 25(c):--the Second derivative curve i.e., the slope of the curve (b) as a function of V to be added

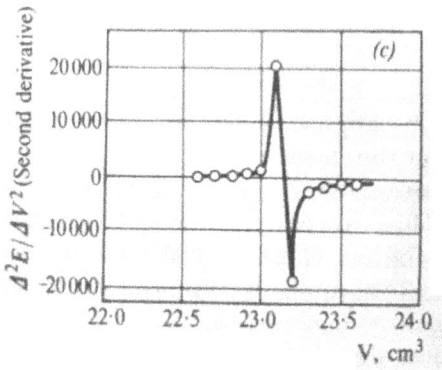

Fig.25(c)

The second derivative becomes zero at the inflexion point and provides a more exact measurement of the equivalence point.

TYPES OF POTENTIOMETRIC TITRATION:--

(1) ACID-BASE TITRATIONS:--

Acid-base titration can be completed potentiometrically by using hydrogen electrode as indicator electrode and calomel electrode as reference electrode.

Acid- base titration can be explained by taking example of titration of 0.1M acetic acid with 0.1M sodium hydroxide solution.

At first known volume of the acetic acid to be titrated is kept in a beaker having automatic stirrer & standard hydrogen electrode. Then it is connected to a calomel electrode through a salt bridge. Further both electrodes are connected to potentiometer which records e.m.f. of the solution. After that sodium hydroxide solution is added from burette into the beaker, then e.m.f. is measured. Finally values of e.m.f are plotted against the ml of the sodium hydroxide solution added.

A curve is obtained as shown in Fig.26

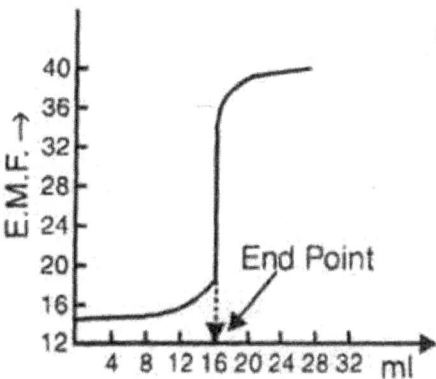

Fig.26.ACID BASE TITRATION

The potential of any hydrogen electrode is given by

$E = E^\theta - 0.0591 \log a_H^+$ at 25°C

where E^θ = standard potential

and pH = $- \log a_H^+$

So, $E = E^\theta + 0.0591$ pH

It can be calculated with the change in electrode potential or e.m.f of the cell which is proportional to the change in pH during titration. The point where e.m.f increases rapidly gives the end point.

(2) COMPLEXOMETRIC TITRATION:--

Complexometric potentiometric titration can be performed in the case of titration of metal ions M^{n+} like calcium, magnesium ions by the use of mercury (II)- EDTA complex HgY^{2-} (EDTA=Na_2H_2Y) in the presence of indicator electrode like mercury/mercury(II)-EDTA complex electrode and calomel electrode as a reference electrode.

A potential corresponding to the half cell can be represented as such ---

Hg/Hg^{2+}, HgY^{2-}, $My^{(n-4)+}$, $M\ n^+$

It can be shown that the potential at equilibrium is given by:--

$$E = E^\theta Hg^{2+}, Hg + \frac{RT}{2F} ln \frac{[HgY^{2--}]}{[MY^{(n-4)+}]} \cdot \frac{K_{MY}}{K_{HgY}} + \frac{RT}{2F} ln[M^{n+}]$$

where K_{MY} and K_{HgY} are the stability constants of the metal-EDTA and mercury-EDTA complexes respectively.

During the process of complexometry potentiometric titration at first 25.0 ml of the metal-ion solution like calcium (approximately 0.05M) is taken in a 250ml pyrex beaker. Then 250ml of the appropriate buffer solution like ammonia buffer solution and 1 drop of 0.25M-mercury-EDTA solution are added. Further titration assembly is placed in position by the use of reference electrode, indicator electrode, magnetic-stirrer and potentiometer.

Then solution is stirred magnetically. After that it is titrated potentiometrically with standard 0.05M-EDTA solution which is added from a burette supported over the beaker. Addition of EDTA solution is reduced to 0.1ml or less as soon as the potential begins to rise. Further wait is made for a steady potential to be established after each addition. Soon after the end point the change of potential with each addition of EDTA becomes samller and only a few large additions need be made. Finally titration curve is plotted against potential in millivolts with volume of standard EDTA solution and then accordingly end-point is evaluated as shown in Fig.27

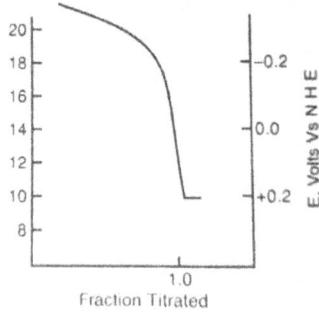

Fig 27

(3) REDOX TITRATION:--

Potentiometric redox titration can be explained by taking example of titration of Iron (II) content of 0.1M ammonium iron(II) sulphate solution with standard potassium dichromate solution by the use of bright platinum electrode as indicator electrode and an standard calomel electrode as reference electrode.

During the process of potentiometric titration, at first 25 ml of the ammonium iron (II) sulphate solution is taken in a beaker. Then 25ml of 2.2M sulphuric acid and 50ml of water are added. After that burette is charged with 0.1N potassium dichromate solution. A capillary extension tube is added.

Further titration assembly is kept in position by the use of reference and standard electrode, salt bridge, potentiometer. Then potassium dichromate solution is added and after each addition e.m.f of the cell is measured.

End point is determined by the use of potential-volume curve and differential method. as shown in Fig 28

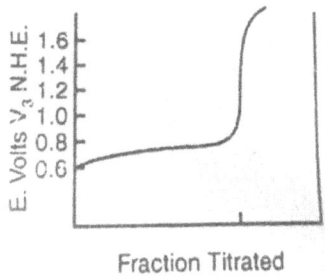

Fig 28

Finally molarity of ammonium iron (II) sulphate solution is calculated.

(4) PRECIPITATION TITRATION:--

Potentiometric Precipitation titration can be explained by taking example of standardization of silver nitrate solution with pure sodium chloride by the use of silver plated platinum wire electrode as indicator electrode and saturated calomel electrode as a reference electrode.

During the process of potentiometric titration, at first 0.1169g of dry A.R. sodium chloride is taken in a beaker. Then 100ml. of water is added and stirred until dissolved.

Then total titration assembly is placed by the use of reference and indicator electrode and potentiometer. After that 0.1M silver nitrate solution is added and after each addition e.m.f of cell is measured.

End-point is determined by the use of potential-volume curve and subsequently molarity of silver nitrate solution is determined as shown in Fig.29

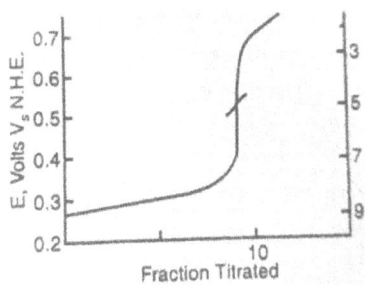

Fig.29

APPLICATION OF POTENTIOMETRIC TITRATION:--

(1) Potentiometric titration is used for studying the effects of calcium, barium and fluorine in detergent manufacturing.

(2) It is used to find out the available elements like nitrate salt, ammonium salt, iodine, calcium, potassium, cyanide present in soils, plant materials etc.

(3) It is used to find out the amount of ammonia, cyanide ion, nitrate salt present in water.

(4) It is used in clinical chemistry to perform blood tests to measure levels of various biochemical parameters.

(5) It is also used to determine the presence of various drugs or toxins in blood or urine.

(c) POLAROGRAPHY:--

Polarography is electrochemical method of analysis where a steadily increasing voltage is applied to a cell having a relatively large mercury anode and a minute mercury cathode (composed of a sucession of small mercury drops falling slowly from a fine capillary tube) and it makes possible to construct a reproducible current-voltage curve.

Electrolyte is a dilute solution of the material to be examined in a suitable medium containing an excess of an indifferent electrolyte known as base or ground solution or supporting electrolyte and used to carry the bulk of the current and raise the conductivity of the solution which ensures that when material is charged then it does not migrate to the dropping mercury cathode.

The value of current flowing through cell at particular voltage is determined with the help of instrument known as POLAROGRAPH and records or curves obtained during analysis known as POLAROGRAMS.

APPARATUS:--

The basic apparatus for Polarographic analysis consists a dropping mercury electrode

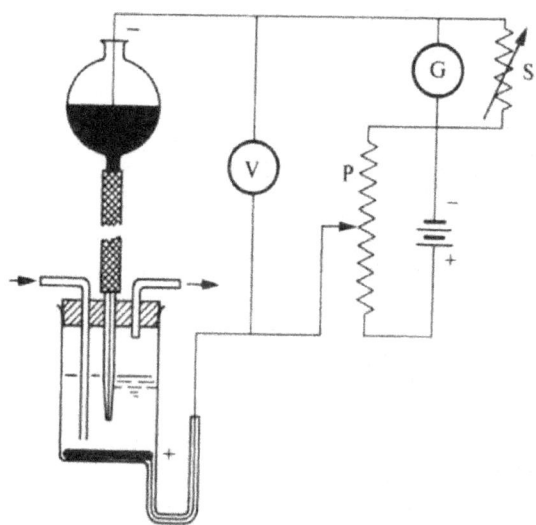

Fig.30 .BASIC APPARATUS USED FOR POLAROGRAPHY

Dropping mercury electrode consists of mercury reservoir from which mercury drops down as small drops through a capillary and acts as cathode and also known as MICRO ELECTRODE.

The anode consists of mercury pool at the bottom of the reservoir. Its area is correspondingly large so it may be regarded as incapable of becoming polarized i.e. its potential remains almost constant in medium containing anions like Cl^-, SO_4^{2-} capable of forming insoluble salts with mercury and it acts as a non- standardized reference electrode.

The exact potential of anode depends upon the nature and concentration of supporting electrolyte. So polarization of the cell is governed by the reactions occurring at the dropping mercury electrode.

Inlet and outlet tubes are provided to the cell for expelling dissolved oxygen from the solution by the passage of an inert gas like hydrogen or nitrogen before starting of polargraphy analysis otherwise polarogram of dissolved oxygen may appear in the current-voltage curve.

P is a Potentiometer by which any e.m.f. up to 3 volts can be applied to the cell gradually as shown in Fig.30

S is a Shunt used for adjusting the sensitivity of Galvanometer G appropriately to the nature and concentration of the substance to be examined.

WORKING:--

Let us consider an external e.m.f is applied to the polarographic cell containing a dilute oxygen-free solution of cadmium chloride; $CdCl_2$.

All positively charged ions present in the solution attract to the negative working electrode i.e., dropping mercury electrode by an electrical force due to the attraction of oppositely charged bodies to each other and by a diffusive force arising from the concentration gradient produced at the electrode surface.

The total current passing through the cell can be considered as sum of these both forces.

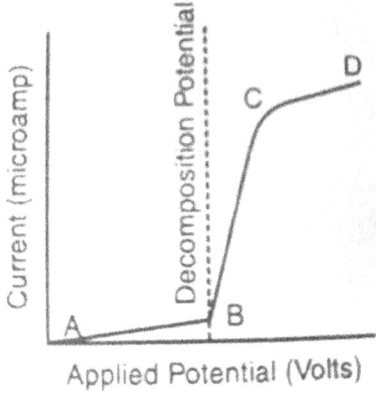

Fig.31. WORKING OF POLAROGRAPHY ANALYSIS

It can be seen that from A to B practically a small current or no current passes through the cell and is known as residual current. At B, the potential of the microelectrode is equal to the deposition potential of the cadmium ions with respect to a metallic cadmium electrode. The current suddenly increases along the curve BC and working electrode becomes depolarized by cadmium ions which are then discharged upon the electrode surface to form metallic cadmium consequently a rapid increase in the current passing through the cell is being observed. At point C the current no longer increases linearly with applied potential but reaches a steady limiting value at the point D. Further no increase in current is observed at higher cathode potentials. Hence, current corresponding to the CD curve is known as limiting current as shown in Fig 31

The difference between the residual current and the limiting current is called the diffusion current and is generally denoted by id.

ILKOVIC EQUATION:--

Ilkovic equation is a relation used in polarography analysis relating the diffusion current(id) and the concentration of the non-polarisable electrode i.e., the substance reduced or oxidized at the dropping mercury electrode (polarisable electrode).

$Id = 607 \, n \, C \, D^{1/2} \, m^{2/3} \, t^{1/6}$

where id = the average diffusion current in microamperes during the life of the drop

n = the number of Faradays of electricity required per mol of the electrolyte reaction

D = the diffusion coefficient of the reducible or oxidisable substance expressed as $Cm^2 \, Sec^{-1}$

C = concentration in milli moles per dm^3

m = the rate of flow of mercury from the dropping electrode expressed in mg per second and

t = drop time in seconds

The constant 607 is a combination of natural constants including the Faraday constant. It is slightly temperature dependent and the value 607 is for 25°C.

The following four factors influence the Ilkovic equation:--

(1) Both m and t shall change with the dimensions of the capillary (its length) and the applied pressure of Hg reservoir to form the drop.

(2) Height of Hg column must be maintained constantly as the drop time solely depends upon the applied pressure by the column of Hg at the tip of DME and analyte solution interface.

(3) Applied voltage for causing possible charges occurring in the prevailing surface tension of a drop at the tip of electrode.

(4) Evidently, the variations in temperature and viscosity must be at bare minimum level because it disturbs the diffusion current most significantly.

FACTORS AFFECTING THE LIMITING CURRENT:--

The factors which affect the current-voltage curve are as follows:--

(1) Residual current

(2) Migration current

(3) Diffusion current

(4) Half wave potential

(1) RESIDUAL CURRENT:--

When mercury drop falls freely into potassium chloride or potassium nitrate then mercury remains electrically uncharged. But if a current-voltage curve is determined for a solution containing ions with a strongly negative reduction potential (e.g., potassium ions) then a small current flows before beginning of decomposition of solution.

This current increases linearly with the applied voltage in the presence of purest air free solution. It cannot be due to reduction of impurities.

So, it can be considered a condenser current or non-Faradic current due to continuous charging of new mercury drops to the applied potential. It is known that metals, when submerged in an electrolyte, are covered with an electrical double layer of positive and negative charged ions. In case of electrolytes containing traces of impurities, a small Faradic current is also superimposed upon the condenser current. It also can be included in the residual current.

Hence, condenser current is due to formation of double layer at the mercury surface and Faraday current is due to the traces of impurities. So it can be written as such:--

Residual current = Faradic current + condenser current

Or,

$i_r = i_f + i_c$

(2) MIGRATION CURRENT:--

Electroative material reaches the surface of the electrode by two processes:--

(i) First process describes migration of charged particles in the electric field caused by the potential difference existing between the electrode surface and the solution.

(ii) Second process is related with the diffusion of particles.

These two processes are governed by migration current.

As per Heyrovsky migration current can be eliminated if an indifferent electrolyte (it conducts the current but does not react with the material under investigation nor at the electrode with the potential range studied).

It can be explained by taking following example:--

Let us suppose an electrolytic solution contains 0.1M potassium ions and 0.005M copper (I) ions.

If we assume that the molar conductivities of K^+ and $½ Cu^{2+}$ are approximately equal, then it follows that 90% of the current is transported to cathode by potassium ions and only 10% by copper ions. Both ions diffuse towards any portion of the solution where a concentration gradient exists but the rate of diffusion becomes slow.

If the concentration of the potassium ions is increased beyond 99% of total cations present, then all the current passing through the cell are transported by potassium ions. In such cases electroactive material reaches the electrode surface only by diffusion.

(3) DIFFUSION CURRENT:--

When an excess of supporting electrolyte is present in the solution then electrical force on the reducible ions is nullified. Because the ions of current and the potential gradient is compressed to a region so very close to the electrode surface and it is no longer operative to attract electro reducible ions. In such condition limiting current is almost solely a diffusion current.

Maximum amount of current is known as diffusion current as shown in Fig.32

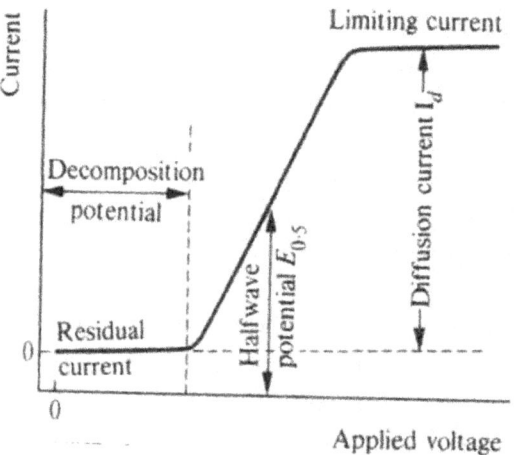

Fig.32:-- DIFFUSION CURRENT

Diffusion current is generally governed by the following Ilkovic equation as such:--

$Id = 607\ n\ CD^{½}\ m^{2/3} + t^{1/6}$

where I_d = diffusion current in micro amperes during the life of the period

n = number of Faradays of electricity required per mole of the electrode reaction

D = Diffusion coefficient of the reducible or oxidisable substance expressed as $cm^2\ sec^{-1}$

C = concentrations in millimoles per dm^3

m = the rate of flow of mercury from the dropping mercury electrode expressed in mg per second

t = drop time in seconds.

It is clear that the diffusion current is directly proportional to the concentration of the electroactive material by keeping all other factors remaining constant.

The Ilkovic equation neglects the effect on the diffusion current of the curvature of the mercury surface. It can be allowed by multiplying the right hand side of the equation by $(1 + AD^{1/2} t^{1/6} m^{-1/3})$,

where A = constant and has a value of 39.

Hence, $i_d = 607 \, n \, CD^{1/2} m^{2/3} t^{1/6} (1 + 39 D^{1/2} m^{-1/3} + t^{1/6})$.

Diffusion current i_d depends upon several factors like temperature, the viscosity of medium, the composition of the base electrolyte, the molecular or ionic state of the electroactive species, the dimensions of the capillary and pressure on the dropping mercury.

(4) HALF WAVE POTENTIAL:--

The usual method of drawing the current voltage curve is to plot the applied e.m.f as abscissae reading in increasing negative values on the right, current is plotted as ordinates as shown in Figure 32, cathodic currents (resulting from reduction) being regarded as positive and anodic currents negative.

The height of the curve (wave height) is the diffusion current and is a function of the concentration of the reacting material.

The potential curve (half wave potential) is characteristic of the nature of the reacting material. This is the essential basis of quantitative and qualitative polarographic analysis.

The potential at the point on the polarographic wave where the current is equal to one half the diffusion current is termed the half wave potential and is designated by $E_{1/2}$

Half-wave potential is a characteristic constant for a reversible oxidation-reduction system and that its value is independent of the concentration of the oxidant in the bulk of the solution.

The half wave potential is also independent of the electrode characteristics. It can be used for the qualitative identification of an unknown substance.

CONSTRUCTION AND WORKING OF DROPPING MERCURY ELECTRODE AND ROTATING PLATINUM ELECTRODE:--

DROPPING MERCURY ELECTRODE:--

Dropping mercury electrode is also known as working or micro electrode. It is used in polarography where mercury continuously drops from a reservoir through a capillary tube (internal diameter 0.03 – 0.05mm) into the solution at an interval of 1 to 5 seconds.

CONSTRUCTION :--

It consists of a mercury reservoir with fine capillary having bore size ranged from 20-50 M and 10-15M long. The capillary is connected to mercury reservoir by rubber tubing as shown in Fig.33

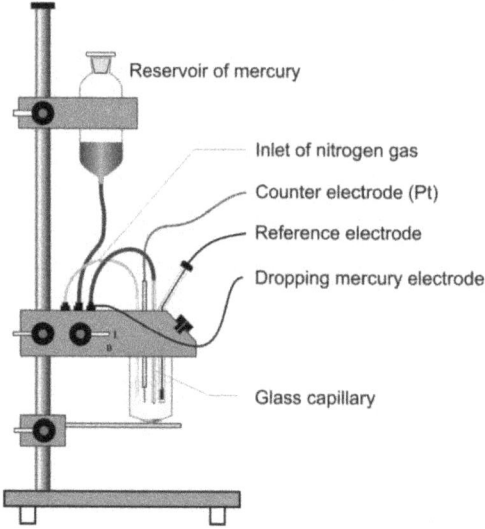

Fig.33:--DROPPING MERCURY ELECTRODE

It also consists a small glass electrolysis cell where unknown solution is placed. The height of mercury reservoir is adjusted in such a way that drop time should be 1-5 seconds.

WORKING:--

Dropping mercury electrode acts as cathode and it is polarisable. The pool of mercury acts as anode and it is non-polarisable electrode. An electrolyte like KCl can be added to analyte solution in the concentration of 50-100 times of sample size. Pure nitrogen or hydrogen gas is bubbled through the solution to remove out oxygen. If analyte solution contains cadmium ions then cadmium ions are discharged at cathode as such

$Cd^{2+} + 2e^- = Cd$

Further gradually increasing voltage is applied to the polarographic cell.

A graph is plotted between voltage applied and current is called polarograph and the apparatus is known as polarogram.

The diffusion current produced is directly proportional to concentration of analyte and same is used in quantitative analysis. The half wave potential is characterstic of compound and usually used in qualitative analysis.

ADVANTAGES OF DROPPING MERCURY ELECTRODE:--

(1) Its surface is smooth, reproducible and continuously renewed.

(2) Mercury forms amalgams (solid solution) with many metals.

(3) The diffusion current assumes a steady value immediately after each charge of applied potential.

(4) The large hydrogen over potential on mercury makes possible the deposition of substances, ions like aluminium ion and manganese (II) ion.

(5) The surface area can be calculated from the weight of the drops.

(2) ROTATING PLATINUM ELECTRODE:--

Rotating platinum electrode can be used at high potential in violating condition of constant in way of increasing sensitivity and also to get steady diffusion current.

CONSTRUCTION:--

The rotating platinum electrode is constructed from a standard mercury seal.

It consists of about 5mm platinum wire having 0.5mm diameter below standard mercury seal by passing through hole as shown in Figure 34

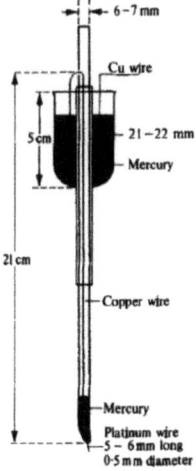

Fig.34 ROTATING PLATINUM ELECTRODE

A wire from mercury seal is connected to the source which applies voltage.

The tubing forms the stem of the electrode which is rotated at a constant speed of 600 rmp.

WORKING:--

Rotating platinum electrode is used as indicator electrode. Supporting electrolyte like KCl i.e., 50-100 times of sample concentration is added to analyte solution. Pure nitrogen gas is bubbled through the solution to expel out the dissolved oxygen.Potential is applied across the electrodes and further process is started.

A graph is plotted between the volume of solution added and diffusion current.Subsequently end point is detected.

APPLICATIONS OF POLAROGRAPHY:--

(1) Application to inorganic compounds:--

Polarography can be used for the estimation of cations like lithium, zinc, nickel etc, and anions like bromate, iodate, nitrite etc in the presence of interfering ions.

(2) Application to organic compounds:--

Polarography is also used to estimate organic compounds like acetone, aldehyde, hydroxylamine, azo compounds etc.

(3)Determination of plant contents:--

Polarography is used for determination of plant contents like essential oils.

(4)It is used to study for the composition of complexes.

(5)It is used for determination of dissolved oxygen in aqueous solution or in organic solvents.

(6)It is also used to find out the percentage purity of medicine like epinephrine, local anaesthetics, analgesics and antipyretics, tetracycline, sulfonamides etc.

www.ingramcontent.com/pod-product-compliance
Lightning Source LLC
LaVergne TN
LVHW070522070526
838199LV00072B/6676